On Grief, Hope, and Motorcycles

A DIARY

Candiya Mann

Candiya Mann
candiya.mann@gmail.com
www.CandiyaMann.com

Cover design by Pete Garceau
Book layout ©2013 Bookdesigntemplates.com

On Grief, Hope, and Motorcycles: A Diary / Candiya Mann. - 1st ed.

ISBN 978-0692589953

10 9 8 7 6 5 4 3 2 1

Contents

For Mike,

who taught me what it was to love and to be loved.

Memorial marker, Unity, Oregon. Photo credit: Brad Everett

When I am silent, I have thunder hidden inside.
—RUMI

There is no path so dark, nor road so steep, nor hill so slippery that other people have not been there before me and survived. May my dark times teach me to help the people I love on similar journeys.
— MAGGIE BEDROSIAN

Preface

I swung the pick-up truck through the steep curves above Pendleton, Oregon, with a smile on my face. It was a sunny August morning, and the clear cerulean sky was a beautiful contrast to the dry grass and rocks of the surrounding hills.

It was going to be another hot day, but the morning felt fresh and comfortable. I put my sunglasses on, unrolled the windows, and let my hair fly free in the breeze. The radio was playing a good country song so I turned it up and sang along at full volume. Why not? Life was good. I felt silly, light, and happy.

Mike – my boyfriend, best friend, love of my life – had returned from the final deployment of his career the day before. He was a submariner in the US Navy so the five years of our relationship had been punctuated by long separations when he went out to sea.

This last deployment had been particularly tough because of the limited communication. He had only been able to send me two emails in the prior two months. I had kept busy with work, travel, and friends, but still...there was only so much distraction possible.

Ours was a relaxed and comfortable relationship, and when

he was away on deployment, I missed the little things the most: The way he'd come up behind me at a party and place his hand on the small of my back, seeing his eyes light up in laughter as we shared a silly joke, telling stories in the evening of how our days had gone, feeling the contentment that radiated from him as he reached out to touch me, when he experienced a moment of pure appreciation for our life together.

Our relationship had long since surpassed my expectations, and I felt a deep-seated sense of wonder and gratitude for it. What would it become in the future? I didn't know, but I looked forward to finding out. This homecoming marked a transition in our relationship, since he would no longer be going out to sea. I knew this change would bring challenges, but I was confident in what we had built together. We did everything we could to make each other happy.

And this was why I was currently driving alone through Oregon – doing what I could to make him happy. I had picked him up from the airport the day before. Pulling into the busy arrivals deck, I had spotted him standing on the curb with his sea bag at his side and a smile in his eyes. My nerves singing with excitement, I quickly stopped the truck and slipped down from the driver's seat. He pulled me in for a long, slow, kiss. Even as I was ready to rush along – no waiting in the loading area, right? – he gently pulled me closer. My nerves about the homecoming started to unknot as a warmth spread through my chest with that kiss. Everything was going to be okay.

This homecoming had coincided with Mike's long-awaited, annual motorcycle road trip with his friends. Mike was an avid motorcyclist. (I loved riding as a passenger but was just a beginner on my own bike.) They had planned the road trip around Mike's deployment schedule, but his return had been delayed past the start of the trip.

So that he wouldn't miss the entire road trip, Mike and I had concocted a plan. I would pick him up at the Seattle airport in his truck with the bike loaded in the back and drive him to Baker City, Oregon, where we would rendezvous with his friends. We would have a night together, and then he'd join them the next morning.

I fully supported this plan. Mike had looked forward to this trip all year. While I missed him already, I knew that this was to be our last extended separation. I could wait a few more days for our vacation together if it meant that he would be able to enjoy this trip with his friends, the highlight of their motorcycling year.

So far, the plan had gone like clockwork. I dropped Mike with his friends that morning, and he was bright-eyed, energetic, and excited for the trip. He gave me a passionate goodbye kiss before donning his helmet, then, laughing, we pantomimed another kiss through his helmet. I took one last photo of the group (Mike, Mark, Brad, and Buz), then they set off south, and I hit the road north, heading back home to Bremerton, Washington, and another week of work at my university job.

An hour into the drive home through Oregon, I was singing in the truck when I heard my phone chime. It was the voicemail notification. I glanced at the phone and felt a sense of foreboding slide over me. Why would Mark be calling from the road now that Mike was back and could call himself? "I need to pull over before listening to this message," I thought. The twisty highway had no shoulders, but there was an exit just ahead. I pulled into the Pendleton rest stop and parked in the first open spot.

Retrieving the message, I heard Mark's halting voice. "I'm so sorry to tell you this…Mike was in an accident…and he didn't make it."

•••

This call marked the end of my world and the beginning of my journey towards peace, redemption, and eventually, joy. Truthfully, there were many times when I did not know if I would survive the journey; it was not a foregone conclusion.

Six months after Mike died, I began to write. An act of desperation, this writing became my salvation. It was an outlet for the intense emotions threatening to devour me from the inside. It was an antidote to the deep isolation, to the sense of constantly having to filter my reality so that it would be acceptable to the outside world.

I began by writing anonymous blog posts – a diary of sorts. As my motorcycle skills improved, I started to take motorcycle trips of my own, recording them in "ride reports", a type of travel blog posted in motorcycle forums. This book is a collection of those blog posts and ride reports, covering roughly a yearlong period that began six months after the accident.

If you had met me during this year, you would have noticed that, on the outside, I managed to carry on a relatively normal life. I worked, met friends for dinner, and traveled. Consider this book to be "the rest of the story". As everyone was complimenting me on my strength on the outside, this book is the uncensored internal experience of my journey through grief.

The stories recounted here are the truth of my experiences. With the grey haze of shock that clouded my brain at that time, I am certain that some of the details are wrong. But this is my best effort to record my journey as I lived it.

I am looking forward to wrapping up this year of writing and releasing it into the world. It will be good for me to let these words fly free. I hope this book will help others as well. Perhaps it will help those in grief see that they are not alone. Perhaps it will land in the hands of someone who finds hope in the pages – even just a thimbleful – enough to help them step away from their own despair.

With this, I welcome you into my world.

Love,

Candiya
(Signing my real name to my writings for the first time)

PS. You may notice that the posts are not entirely in chronological order. I rearranged them slightly to help the narrative flow more smoothly – and also because I wrote a few pieces before starting the blog.

PPS. I have to apologize for the quality of the photos. When I started writing, I was not setting out to write a book but just to record my journey. I snapped photos along the way with my cell phone, which worked for the blog but didn't produce print-quality images. Nevertheless, I hope they help illustrate my journey.

Part One:
Desperation

February – September, 2013

CHAPTER 1

A beginning, finally

February 17, 2013

On August 22, 2012, my boyfriend, Mike, died in a motor-cycle accident. Within the first three days, I knew that I wanted to write a blog. Over the ensuing days and weeks, then weeks and months, I made notes of blog topics on my phone. I drafted a couple posts on my tablet. I wrote an introductory blog post on a motorcycle forum. I even opened an account on Word-Press. Yet I did not blog.

This beginning already feels different than those false starts. I now know the purpose and personality that this blog will take. There is no other place where I can be 100% honest about this experience, this crazy, brutal, sad, absurd grief journey. In my regular life, my persona is wise and understanding. My Face-book posts are honest but vaguely uplifting. But this, *my blog*, will be the place where there is no need to censor myself. This will be my safe space where there is no need to protect those around me.

In my grief class, they likened grief to being dropped in a wilderness, a jungle, and having to find your way out. I think that's a very apt description. I have no idea how long the journey will take or where it will take me. But you're welcome to join me for the ride if you're so inclined.

Today is February 17, 2013, almost six months since Mike died, and I am beginning.

CHAPTER 2

Six months

February 22, 2013

Six months since the accident. Six months since you died. Six months with no kisses, hugs, conversation, adventures, rides. Six months with no email, Facebook posts, PNWrider private messages, Kik Messenger chats, Skype video calls.

Six of the hardest months of my life. Getting that call, calling your mom, giving your uniforms to the master chief for the funeral and the cremation, walking the accident site, writing the obituary and eulogy, attending the memorial service, sorting your stuff, watching the Navy pack it up and cart it away, selling your bikes, listening to them start and ride away, riding in our track day, going back to work, continuing to work even though it feels pointless, attending lawyer appointments, receiving letters-statements-documents, page after page with those hated words in the upper corner, "Michael James Bartlett, deceased", peeling myself off the damn couch day-after-day, forcing myself to go to sleep/go to work.

But also...

Six months of the most amazing generosity. Six months of

my shattered heart opening up and receiving, receiving, receiving unlooked-for love from all corners of the world. Cards and flowers and gifts pouring in: a hand-painted watercolor and poem from a colleague, a journal, a plaque with a comforting quote, photos. Friends, family, acquaintances, and people I'd never met before sharing their own stories of loss and grief, being open and vulnerable and real before me. So many people lifting me up, propping me up, stepping in over and over again at exactly the right moment. I am humbled with gratitude.

Six months. Often, it still feels as if you're on deployment. In six months you should have been home for three months and out to sea for three months, your regular schedule. Last year, you returned home from deployment yesterday, February 21st.

In 2012, you were home February 21-May 13 and August 21-22. It wasn't enough. Not *nearly* enough. And it would never be enough. I rail against the fact that you are not coming home again. Not. Ever. Coming. Home. Again. I hate it, loath it, protest it, refuse to accept it, beat my fists against it in fury, desperation, fear, sadness, grief. I throw myself against the giant immutable wall of death, and I am as nothing. I am powerless and frail against this opponent. I break myself against this wall again and again. I cannot win, but I also cannot accept this yet.

Six months, and I am becoming... What? I do not know. But I am transforming, the new me built upon the crumbles of the old.

Six months, and all I know for sure is that I miss you. I wish the past six months could be taken back, like the snap of a tape measure retracting. But it can't so I am marching forward, resolutely, with you in my heart.

A sign?

February 12, 2013

Yesterday, I went for a walk with a friend who was at the accident and asked him to tell me the story of the accident day. He told me the full story, at least as he remembered it. I'm sure the guys were in shock as much as I was, and that affects your memory.

As we walked, it wasn't the brutal parts of the story that affected me: hearing about how Mike's head was swollen, and blood was coming out of his mouth and ears. I pictured the guys frantically trying to remove his helmet and keep his mouth clear from the sticky warm blood that wouldn't stop. No, the part that almost undid me, that made my chest quiver where I had carefully guarded it before this conversation, was when he described the highway patrol officer returning to his car, retrieving a blanket from his trunk, and placing it over Mike.

The sweetness of that image, how you place a blanket over

your sleeping child, your sleeping lover. The starkness of how I imagine that image. Mike's body so large and solid in life becoming just a small patch of blanket under that sweeping sky, that broad beautiful landscape. In my mind's eye, the camera pans away, and it's a silent view of the guys standing there, useless, their bikes, the highway patrol officer, and other emergency vehicles.

The finality of that blanket. Soft and gentle and brutal and sad. Crushing, really.

After that walk, I went for my first real ride since Mike's birthday two months ago. My thoughts were heavy as I tried to come to terms with the story of the accident day. My route took me down misty, gray, twisty back roads. I stopped after about 45 minutes at an elementary school. Just sat there staring at the empty playing fields, feeling bleak. Trying to come to terms with the images in my head. Trying to find the motivation to get on my bike and make my way home. Just waiting...for what, I didn't know.

Just then, I heard other bikes approach and turned to see two bikes pulling into the parking lot. It was a couple out riding. She was on the twin of my bike - same color scheme and everything - the first CBR250R I'd seen in the county. He was on a Yamaha dual sport. Nice young couple. We started to talk, and I noticed that she hadn't turned off her light. I pointed it out to her. "You don't want to get stuck out here," I said. "Oh," she responded. "It's okay, I have him," gesturing at her boyfriend. I smiled and nodded and sternly pushed down my wistful response to that offhand reliance on her partner.

I wondered how I looked to them, a woman out for a ride alone. Maybe I looked self-reliant, experienced. The truth is that I missed my riding partner. He would have been there with me if he was still here. (Well, maybe he still is with me, but you know what I mean.)

But strangely, this encounter lifted my spirits. After they left, I headed home with a lighter heart. My bike felt zippy beneath me, and I enjoyed the corners of the twisty road home.

It was only later that it occurred to me that this couple could have been a sign. What are the chances that as I stood there waiting, feeling bleak and hopeless, the first twin of my bike I've seen in a year should come riding up, as part of a couple? I don't know what it meant or if it was a sign. But I hope so.

CHAPTER 4

Single...but not

February 26, 2013

Sometimes I find myself going round and round, like that game where you pull the petals off a flower while reciting, "He loves me; he loves me not". In my case, it's "I'm single, but I'm not, but I am, but I'm....not".

Of course, if I stand up and count the people in this relationship, there's only me. One. That's pretty definitively single. But the other meaning of "single" is "available". And that does not fit.

Once, while Mike was on deployment, a girlfriend described me as "her faux-single friend". I found it amusing at the time, though it may describe me better now.

So...on the topic of faux-singlehood, I thought I'd share some stories.

On New Year's Eve, I went dancing with a girlfriend. It was my first time dancing since the accident, and I felt a little trepidation. I decided to view the outing as a social experiment. How would people react if I was honest about my situation? I decided that if anyone asked my relationship status, I'd tell the truth.

Shortly after arriving, I danced with a nice young man. Taking a break from the dance floor, we exchanged the basics. He was 26 and in the Army. When he asked if I had a boyfriend or husband, I said, "No, my boyfriend died a few months ago in a motorcycle accident." He drew away, looked at me with concern, and respectfully asked if he should leave. I reassured him that no, it was okay, I was there to dance. We danced off and on throughout the night, until he left with his friends shortly after midnight.

At another point during the night, I was dancing by myself when a guy came up and started to dance in front of me. He asked my name, and we started to dance together. He leaned forward and yelled in my ear, "What's your situation? Do you have a boyfriend?" I responded, "Do you really want to know my situation?" After he said, "yes", I told him that my boyfriend had died in a motorcycle accident a few months ago.

I waited for his response. He kept dancing then said, "Your boyfriend is SO lucky." Huh? He must not have heard. Awkwardly, I leaned forward and yelled in his ear. "I don't think you heard me. He's DEAD. He died in a motorcycle accident a few months ago." This got a response.

The poor guy JUMPED backwards away from me and stood stock still on the dance floor. With wild eyes, he asked me, "What do I do? What do I do?" "It's okay", I said. "Let's just dance." But he just stood there, completely freaked out, repeating, "What do I do?" until I finally said, "I don't know!" It's not like I have a handbook for how to handle social situations after a death.

I tried again, "Look, let's just dance." I felt bad for freaking him out. He agreed, and we began to dance again. A few minutes went by before he started to croon, "Your boyfriend's SO lucky.

He's just SO lucky." That was it for me. This situation had just passed my weirdness tolerance. I stepped back, said, "Thank you for the dance," and left.

A month later, another funny situation came up. I stopped at the local brewery for a beer after work. The place was empty, except for me at the bar and four people at a table. An older man joined me at the bar and started to make conversation. He had a weird vibe, but I thought that I should be polite so we talked. In our short conversation, he managed to mention his houses, boats, and "investments". He also kept dropping comments about my "husband", fishing for information. I let those comments slide by.

Finally, he decided a more direct approach was needed. He looked me up and down twice then asked, "So I notice you don't have a ring. Are you married?" Though his gaze made my skin crawl, I answered politely with my (now) normal response. "No, my boyfriend died in a motorcycle accident a few months ago." He turned to look at his beer. "Oh, that's too bad," he mumbled. A few moments went by before he brightened and said, "I have a motorcycle too. I can do 'stand-ups' on it and everything!"

"Mmmm", I said noncommittally. Seriously? Did he just try to use my boyfriend's death as an opening for picking me up? As he continued to talk, explaining how fast his bike was and hinting heavily that he could take me as a passenger, I didn't bother to tell him that I could ride. I just breathed an internal prayer of thanks that I could give myself what I needed on a bike. (Thank you for teaching me, Mike!)

Postscript...

A week later, I shared this story with a girlfriend. After shaking her head, she said, "That's awful. But I bet you get that a lot from motorcycle riders." I was quick to correct her. "Actually, no. The motorcycle community has been so respectful and supportive. I haven't had a single inappropriate comment from a motorcycle rider."

Of course, this guy could ride a motorcycle, but he wasn't a *motorcycle rider*. In my mind, the line between the two categories is clear and definitive. Being a motorcycle rider means much more than being able to operate the controls.

CHAPTER 5

Non-PC confessions

February 27, 2013

Part One

I admit it. I am not okay with the organ donor part of this experience. I know that it should give me comfort to know that even in his death, Mike was still helping others. And not just a few individuals but almost 50. At least, that's what the letters from the organ donor agencies said.

I can picture Mike marking the organ donor box on his driver's license. Practical in the extreme, he'd have shrugged and said, "If I can't use it, might as well help someone else." It was a simple decision for him, I'm sure. And I can't say that I wish he'd chosen differently. Of course, it's true. He had no need for his body anymore. A different decision would not have spared his life.

And yet...

I loved his body. I loved touching him and the communication we shared through touch.

People think of organ donation as somehow clean. The doctors will take discrete organs from inside of you but leave the essential "you" intact. This is not always the case, as I learned.

Mike donated his skin, leg bones, and corneas.

This is horrifying to me. The person I loved most in the world without his skin? How do you even get to leg bones? Losing his eyes? The damage to his body from the accident could have been nothing compared to the desecration of this harvesting.

A few days after the accident I had a nightmare, one that has not been repeated, thank God. In it, he was reaching for me sexually as his body pulled apart like wet tissue paper. I said no in horror, and as I turned away, his hand tore off with me.

I am left with deeply unresolved feelings about the damage to his body, the loss of the physical connection to him.

Part Two

In many ways, the loss of the physical Mike is harder than the loss of the spiritual Mike. At first, I found this shameful. Shouldn't I miss the spirit more than the body?

Over time, I've grown to understand this better. Before his last trip home, he had been on deployment for over three months. In the final two months, he was only able to send me two emails. While it wasn't easy, I was used to our separation, used to feeling his emotional support from afar. I still feel a spiritual connection with him. That part is changed but not entirely lost.

But the physical. I missed him intensely during this deployment. There was so much anticipation for his return. It was the last deployment of his career, the final extended time apart. He died 25 hours after returning.

Many people have said to me, "At least you had that last night with him." Yes, I will be forever grateful that we had that night together, that our last words were loving, that we were

100% solid, that there was no unfinished business at the end.

But for the physical side, I don't think most people understand. Three months of longing and several weeks of heavy anticipation are not sated in one night. That night simply whet the appetite and spurred the anticipation for our vacation, which was to come after his motorcycle road trip.

Let's be frank here. Of course, sex is a part of the physical. But it's more than that. My most intense fantasy since the accident? Reaching out and touching his warm, solid leg through the soft flannel of his pj's. That's it. The fantasy doesn't progress past that point. I simply want to be able to reach out and touch him. It is a simple desire but one that is deep, intense, and destined to be unrequited.

There's another level of the physical: the desire to be in his physical presence. I wish I could just turn to him, tell a story from my day, and see his eyes light up in laughter. We took such pleasure from each other's company.

One time when he had a port call, we video chatted. After catching up, we played truth or dare. His last "truth" question was what I missed most about him while he was on deployment. I considered various answers but finally told him that I'd have to think about it. In my next email, I wrote that what I missed most was "the essence" of him, simply being with him. His email response closed with, "I look forward to returning the essence of me to your loving arms."

I missed the physical him so deeply before he was even dead. And this longing has not diminished since his loss.

Postscript...

December 29, 2014

I found out much later that the organ donation process is not as invasive as I had envisioned. Corneas can be collected with just the thinnest sliver; leg bones are replaced with prosthetic bones; and generally, only a few layers of skin are collected.

Before learning these facts, my mind had conjured horrible, gruesome images of the organ donation. Thankfully, I have been able to release those, and they have been replaced by mental images that show that the process was respectful. I still don't like to think of Mike's organ donation, but this news has been a comfort to me.

CHAPTER 6

Monet

January 10, 2013

In Washington DC for work, with a couple free hours, I made a beeline for my favorite museum, the National Gallery of Art. I like visiting this museum alone because my pace would drive any companion batty. I'm not there to float slowly past the artwork, gravely considering each piece.

No, I stride through the halls until I find something that makes me feel something, then I stop stock still. The magnetic pull draws me so close the painting doesn't make sense anymore. It becomes a maze of brushstrokes, ridges and valleys built of paint. Then I push myself backwards and consider the image as it pulls itself together with distance. What does it tell me at three feet, at six feet? I sit down and make friends with it.

This day, it was a Monet that caught me. It sucked the breath out of my chest and wouldn't let it free. A thought rang in my head, "I want to be there." I could smell the dank air, rich with rotting plants and damp soil. Feel the still, humid air, heavy on my bare skin.

I pictured myself crawling through the frame. But where, exactly, did I want to be? There was no dry land in the image. Would I lie on the bridge? No, that would be unsatisfying. I needed to immerse myself in this landscape. I could float on that water. Or even better, I could be beneath the water. Yes, that's it. I want to lie beneath the water looking up, like a burial with a view.

The world demands action. It picks at me, pulls on me, pokes me, prods me. Sometimes, I just want to be still. I want to find a Monet landscape, a lazy warm summer field where the only sound is the faraway buzzing of bees. Somewhere the world would pass me by, would just let me...be.

The Japanese Footbridge *by Claude Monet, 1899, National Gallery of Art*

CHAPTER 7

Safety

March 3, 2013

A couple nights ago, I had a minor meltdown, calling a friend in tears because I didn't know how to do motorcycle maintenance. It was faintly ridiculous...but also not. In my grief class, we discussed how losing a loved one could also mean losing whatever they provided or meant to you. For me, losing Mike meant losing my safety. This plays out in numerous ways. We'll get back to motorcycle maintenance in just a bit.

In the middle of the night, sometimes I hear strange noises. When Mike was in bed with me, I felt safe. Now I bargain with the phantom intruders in my head. "You can have the kitchen," I think to them. (My phantom intruders have ESP, apparently.) "Just leave me the bedroom." I lie in bed listening for the next noise, knowing that even if it is something bad, there's nothing I can do about it. It gives me a sense of fatalism.

After Mike's death, several people asked if I was going to get a gun. I don't know if having a gun would make me feel safer. Or if it would make me safer in reality. If push came to shove, I don't know if I could actually squeeze the trigger. Maybe I'd simply provide the intruder with a convenient weapon.

One night after hearing a thump in the kitchen, I thought irritably, "I don't need a gun; I need a cat. That way, when I hear a strange noise, I can just blame the damn cat. That'd make me feel safer." I know it's silly and that it wouldn't actually make me safer. But it makes me smile, at least.

Another way that I lost my sense of safety is that I lost my safe space in the world. Everyone needs a space where they can let down their guard. Where someone else can carry the burdens of life. Where they can be rejuvenated and loved. My safe space was defined by the boundary of Mike's arms. Without those arms, that space does not exist. This breaks my heart. It's also incredibly fatiguing.

And finally, back to motorcycle maintenance. On Friday I went for a ride in the rain. I know that your chain can rust if you don't take care of it after a rain ride so I tried what a friend had suggested. I sprayed it with WD40. Of course, I didn't know how to get the bike up on stands so I applied some WD40, moved the bike forward, applied some more, and hoped for the best. I knew this was inadequate though because there was no way to be sure I covered the entire chain. After a text exchange with a friend, I realized that WD40 wasn't the same as chain lube. This was a fairly minor point, but it sent me over the edge.

When I went on a ride with Mike, I'd be putting on my gear, and he'd be knocking around the garage prepping the bikes. When he was on deployment, he was only gone a few months, and I knew he'd be able to correct any damage I did with my neglect of maintenance. But now he's gone. If I can't figure out how to do this stuff, it will become a safety issue. And I have NO idea where to start. I understand the theory of mechanical stuff, but how to physically do anything...I'm completely lost.

It's overwhelming. It makes me feel foolish, pathetic, stupid, and helpless.

This isn't stuff I was supposed to have to know. We took care of each other, picking up tasks according to our strengths, and motorcycle maintenance was Mike's responsibility. He left me unprepared. If I am going to keep riding, I can't ignore this task. In order to be safe, I need to at least be able to clean and lube my chain, put my bike on stands, maybe change my oil, and just be able to look at the bike and spot any burgeoning problems. I need to learn the basics of motorcycle maintenance so I can provide my own safety.

CHAPTER 8

"We will be okay"

March 7, 2013
Drafted on a flight from San Francisco to Seattle

After a really down week last week, feeling negative and just very alone, this week was lightened. What a relief.

But last night, as I sat in my sad little motel room in San Francisco with the cracked window, I could feel my mood darkening again. I realized that I am nervous about going to Kansas for Mike's burial. It occurred to me, finally, that I'd be at Mike's grave, with his urn.

Sitting in the motel room, I felt a creeping fear come over me. I almost texted a friend and asked him to tell me that it was going to be okay. But then I thought it was a stupid request so I didn't. I just waited for the feeling to pass - or at least, until I got tired enough to sleep.

Today, when exiting a restaurant after a business lunch, I stopped stock still when I spotted the framed saying over the fireplace mantle. "WE WILL BE OKAY," it said in block letters. I don't know what it meant, but it felt like the universe was giving me what I can't seem to ask for.

A recurring theme lately has been not being able to ask for support or even knowing who to ask. I have no problem connecting with friends when we're already together in person. But I don't have people I'm comfortable calling when I'm alone, in tears. Whether it's the middle of the night, and they're asleep, or the middle of the day, and they're busy, it just doesn't seem right to call. It seems like it would be intrusive, and if they didn't have time for me, it would hurt.

Last weekend, I went to the Euro Moto Show. I went alone, and it was sad. A year ago, I was there with Mike and a whole group of riders. This year, I wandered the floor solo, talking to the salespeople. I could feel the grief growing inside me, until I finally left the show at 1:00 pm. I sat in my car in the parking lot and wheezed and teared up. I took out my phone but couldn't think of anyone to call or text so I put it away. Nothing to do but get some lunch so I drove off. It's amazing how you can carry on through your days, even while bowed under the weight of grief.

CHAPTER 9

Whiny little bitch

March 9, 2013
Drafted on the flight from Seattle to Kansas

Yesterday, a work friend stopped by my desk. "Got any big plans this weekend?" she asked. "I'm going to Kansas for Mike's burial," I answered. She gave me the "huh?" look. I explained that Mike had been cremated, and his family wanted him placed in the cemetery with his grandparents, in the small town in Kansas that was home for four generations of their family. Spring break was when everyone was available so we're flying in from around the country this weekend.

Part of me is like, "Seriously? It's been six months, and my life is still not normal. Who spends their weekend going to their boyfriend's burial? This is not normal." Then I feel like a whiny little bitch for complaining. But then again, if anything is worth complaining about, wouldn't it be your boyfriend's burial? That there has to be one at all?

On the other hand, I've been looking forward to this weekend for months. It will be good to see Mike's family - his parents and sisters. It will be good to meet the family members I've only heard of. I'm looking forward to hearing more stories about Mike and sharing some stories of my own. It will just be good not to feel so alone in this grief journey.

I'm curious to see the headstone. It's been in the works for months. It's being made by hand by the only monument engraver near the small town in Kansas. Last November, his family was faxing headstone options to me at work to get my opinion. (Just another way that the oddities of this experience seeped into my daily life over a period of months. Normal people also don't have their boyfriend's headstone options faxed to them at work.) I'm interested to see how it turned out. I hope that it's a beautiful and fitting tribute.

I have mixed feelings about the grave. It's scary and final. But I also want to see his final resting place. Just as it helped me to know what the accident site was like, it will be good to face this too.

Several people have asked if this trip is "bringing stuff up again." No, I haven't been through the graveside part of this experience yet. It's bringing up new stuff.

"Another step forward," I've been saying to myself. The saying has a faintly positive tinge. This is true. But the fuller phrase that just played through my head is "one more step through the chamber of horrors." And this is also true.

One of my favorite movies is *Shawshank Redemption*. Near the end, the voiceover intones, "Andy Dufresne, who crawled through a river of shit and came out clean on the other side." Maybe this grief journey will parallel this.

A couple days ago I ran across a different image of grief. In a book review of a grief memoir, the writer described the grief journey not as emerging from a tunnel into the light but as emerging from an oil slick, tarred and feathered for life. And I think this is true too. My love for Mike and my loss of Mike will always be a part of me.

Postscript...

I must admit that, even while flying towards Kansas and Mike's burial, the "normal" that I crave isn't the cessation of memorials and tributes to him. No, the normal I am waiting for is for him to come home so we can put this all behind us. Grief must be a type of insanity. I simultaneously believe that he is dead and that he is coming home.

CHAPTER 10

Kansas

March 12, 2013
Drafted on the flight from Kansas to Seattle

I don't know how to describe this trip; there were such highs and lows.

Highs:

- Meeting Mike's family and being welcomed as part of them.
- Playing cards with them every night and laughing my head off.
- Holding Mike's cousin, Adelina, (four-years-old) in my lap while playing poker badly as she helped by reading off my cards out loud.
- Seeing Mike's grandfather's motorcycle, which I had heard so much about.

Memories:

Sunday, 1:30 pm: Memorial service. Sitting in the pew in the small, one room country church where Mike's uncle was the minister. The piano and organ side-by-side, out of tune with each other yet perfect. Everything about the situation perfect. Except my heart, breaking, breaking, breaking. Trying to breathe. Holding the box of tissues on my knees.

Sunday, 2:30 pm: Graveside. At the cemetery, 28 degrees and blowing hard, bitterly cold. Sitting in that row of metal folding chairs before the bier holding the brass urn and marble vault, with the flowers at the base. Mike's sisters with their arms entwined in mine, their hands covering mine in my lap, while I shuddered with cold, with grief. The minister said, "We are here to say our final goodbyes to Mike." It still makes me cry to write those words. And really, it could not be more final. The cemetery, the urn, the vault. The family pressed against me and the crowd in dark clothing huddled behind us.

Sunday, 10:30 pm: Sitting on the couch at the house later that evening rocking and crying. His sister asked if I was okay. I shrugged and said, "It is what it is. You know." The truth is that I had never felt such pain. I didn't know that you could experience such pain and not die from it. Being with Mike's family made him seem so close, reminded me of him so clearly and strongly, all the good that he was, everything that he brought to my life. The staggering loss.

Monday, 11:00 am: Visiting the monument company to see the headstone. It was finished, but the weather didn't cooperate so it hadn't been erected at the cemetery yet. Just one nice man running the business. He took us through his workshop and out the back door to see the headstone, huddled with a number of others against the back of the building. It was the only time in Kansas that I was moved to ask for a picture of myself. There are three photos of me with my arm over the headstone, the most awkward photos you've ever seen. Do you smile or not in this situation? Hell, I don't know. I was walking and talking normally until a "griefburst" hit me, as they had throughout the weekend. Just a random fit of tears.

Tuesday noon: Standing in the quiet cemetery this afternoon, with the only sound the wind whooshing past. Wandering through the old headstones, dating back to the early 1800's. Hearing the crunch of the packed thatch grass beneath my feet. The patchy clouds opened and closed, and the field went light and dark, light and dark.

Forcing myself to recognize that the mound of broken earth was Mike. Mike in his brass urn, within the marble vault, beneath the rich earth, below the spray of flowers. Mike with the Bartlett headstones beside him: his grandparents and great grandparents. His parents will join him someday. This tiny, sweet, historic cemetery in this land that his family farmed and farms still, though he hadn't lived here since he was a babe.

While it would not have been my first choice of where to place him, he belongs here. I see it now. He belongs in this quiet, still, quaint, beautiful setting, surrounded by his family. I am glad that I came. I am glad that I know his final resting place.

Mike's grandfather's bike

Stringtown Cemetery, Burlington, Kansas

CHAPTER 11

After the burial

March 28, 2013

The burial was much harder than I expected. I had thought it might be a wistful, soft, gentle goodbye. My experience couldn't have been farther from this. It was brutal. It pierced me to the core. It felt like a Band-Aid being ripped off a wound, tearing away my hope.

Standing in the cemetery at the graveside service, next to the urn and broken earth, I felt despair. He would not be coming home. When I returned to the cemetery with his mom and sister for a final visit, the understanding began to settle over me that this was his new home.

Two days ago, his mom sent a photo of the headstone, now placed in the cemetery. It hit me like a physical blow to the chest. It sounded like the doors to the cells in Alcatraz closing, with an echoing thud of finality.

The headstone is shocking in its solidity, in its simplicity. There is no escaping it. His name, birth date, death date, and "in loving memory" at the bottom. My eye wants to slide off of it, but there is nothing to distract me, nothing to soften this image.

The letters are carved deeply into the granite. There is nothing tentative about it, nothing that intimates, "Oh, we may have made a mistake." This headstone will endure for decades.

As hard as it is to deal with the reality of the headstone, it is also comforting. There is something about the broad solidity of its shape that reminds me of his chest. It anchors him even more firmly there, in the cemetery.

This is a fundamental shift in my heart. If he is there, he can't be here. If he is there, he can't be coming home. For six months, I have struggled to believe that he is not coming back. No matter how hard I tried, I just couldn't get that understanding to stick. Even walking the accident site and bringing back pieces of his bike didn't do it.

The graveside ceremony, cemetery visit, and headstone have given me this gift. This is not a gentle gift. Not one that I want. I would reject it emphatically, thoroughly, defiantly...if there was any alternative. But there isn't. There isn't any path out of this jungle of grief but through the heart.

CHAPTER 12

A gift

March 24, 2013
Drafted on a flight from Washington, DC to Seattle

Today, before heading home from a conference in DC, I met a friend from grad school for lunch. We hadn't seen each other in about 10 years. I thought it would be a pleasant, casual, catch-up meal. How wrong I was.

I rode the escalator up from the subway, emerging into daylight at the busy, urban, upscale Dupont Circle neighborhood. Moments later, I saw her striding towards me. Her eyes lit up as she saw me, and I felt my heart open. It felt like an orange unzipping its peel and turning inside out to show the perfect, juicy, vulnerable sections within. We hugged, and it felt like hugging a sister.

Almost immediately, we started talking about grief. She asked about Mike, and I learned about the loss of her mom this past year. Our conversation was gripping. We two were so hungry for connection, to be understood, to learn each other's stories, to swallow each other's griefs and reflect them back. At brunch, the waiter had to return three times before we finally forced ourselves to pause and order. Our conversation was wide ranging, punctuated with tears, laughter, and packages of tissues and hand wipes. We shared photos, stories, and confessions.

These days, I censor myself quite a bit. I try to protect those around me from pain (if they're too close to Mike's loss) and from awkwardness (if they're not). I don't talk about him with some of his closest friends because they are trying to put the accident behind them. I try to be polite and sensitive. Eventually though, it gets to be too much.

Last week, my counselor said, "You've been traumatized by this loss." Yes! Sometimes I say to myself, "I'm the one who's damaged, and I need to protect your happy ass so I don't burst your happy little bubble??" Ha! Bitter much? For example, last week a friend posted on Facebook, complaining that the snow was fantastic, but her husband wouldn't take her snowboarding. I so wanted to add a comment of, "Aaaaaannnnnd, this is where you count your blessings." But I didn't because it would have been rude and mean. Besides, her reality is just as valid as mine.

Another example: about a month ago at a birthday party, a friend excitedly shared a spiritual breakthrough she had recently made. She gushed, "I'm not even afraid of death! It was the last thing, and I've totally let it go." I smiled and nodded and carefully didn't say, "Yes, you may have released the fear of your own death, but let's talk about your sons. How would you feel if you got a call that one of them had died?" I didn't say anything because kind, polite people don't say things like that at birthday parties. And it would have served no purpose other than making her feel bad.

But you can see that with occasion after occasion of censoring myself, the frustration mounts. The feeling of isolation grows. The conversation today with my friend was so needed.

It was such a release to speak candidly, to not have to explain the grief experience, which can never truly be explained. Trying to explain grief is like trying to describe flavors to a person without taste buds. No matter how florid and descriptive you are and how much they want to understand, they will never fundamentally "get it" without being able to experience taste themselves.

While we only had a couple hours together, which was certainly not enough time to cover everything about our lives today, not to mention the 10 years of history, we parted ways feeling comforted. The pent up frustration in my chest has released. I am so grateful. This commonplace event, a simple lunch with a friend, turned out to be a priceless gift.

CHAPTER 13

On riding two-up

April 1, 2013

I'm not ashamed to admit it. I love riding two-up. Unabashedly. This is not "riding bitch". I am not a sack of potatoes on the back of the bike – extra weight whose only purpose is to deaden the bike's handling. I am not a victim – helpless at the hands of the rider. I am a partner in the ride.

Why I Love It

Once while playing truth or dare, Mike asked what I loved so much about riding two-up with him. I thought for a bit then told him my three favorite moments in a ride:

1) Waking early on a crisp, bright, fresh summer morning. Climbing on the bike to meet his friends for the ride, a whole day's adventure stretching before us.

2) On any ride, you have the ride-to-the-ride, then you have The Ride. I love the transition between the two. The moment when the lead bike takes off, and it's on. It's not a race, it's a dance. I can feel his attention contract and the world come into sharp focus. His quads and core engage, and he leans forward.

This is where the rhythm of the ride begins. I am fully engaged. Head over the inside shoulder. Look up through the turn! Outside shoulder or breasts touching his back at all times, allowing me to follow his lean, making us as one. Elbows on my knees or pressing against his core. Weight the inside peg. Brake, brake, brake – *squeeze* the legs and push on the tank to keep myself off his back. It is extremely physical, and I love it.

I have rarely felt such pure, unadulterated joy as I did while riding in tandem with Mike. The moments where the road unfurls like a curled ribbon before us, luscious dark pavement. The two of us as one with the bike, with each other. Glimpses of glorious views, between one corner leading us to the next then the next. I am greedy, a glutton for the road, for that moment, for that feeling, for that flow. In that moment, it seems that I can never be satisfied, that there will never be enough.

But eventually, it is time to turn around, leading us to number three...

3) The ride home, with sunset falling. Tired, but the good kind of tired. The cobwebs and stresses of daily life scrubbed away. Both of us mellow and relaxed, just cruising, his friends in formation around us. He sits up, a hand on his hip, then reaches back, allows his arm to fall across my leg and squeezes. It's a perfect moment.

I never had a chance to ask him what he liked best about riding two-up with me. It was on my list of questions that I planned to ask during truth or dare after his last return.

Grief isn't about mourning a single loss. It's a million tiny cuts – and larger ones too. One of those cuts is the loss of our two-up rides.

What It Taught Us

Riding two-up gave us many gifts. It taught us to trust each other and how to work together as a cohesive team. It taught us how to communicate without words, through touch. While on the bike, we knew if the other person was happy, excited, focused, tired, frustrated, and more. Of course, this all translated off the bike too: the trust, the teamwork, the communication.

For example, one night we were relaxing at home, watching TV and surfing the motorcycle forum. He was facing forward on the couch, and I was curled up with my back against his side and his arm crooked across my chest. It was our favorite "relax and cuddle on the couch" position.

We couldn't see each other's faces while sitting this way. Still, when a moment of melancholy hit me, he immediately asked if everything was okay. I was flummoxed. How the heck did he know that my mood had changed from looking at the back of my head?

Of course, the back of my head hadn't told him a damn thing. It was the intuition and communication built up from hours and hours together on the bike. We were in tune with one another. Our dance on the back of the bike made us wonderful partners in life.

Our helmets

CHAPTER 14

Facing fear

April 4, 2013

A few months after the accident, I signed up for adult hip hop classes at a dance studio, an alternative workout from the spin classes that Mike and I used to take together. I've mentioned the dance class to a number of people and generally get the same response: "Oh, that sounds like fun! I'd love to take a class like that, but I'm not good at dancing." This reply makes my eyes cross. It's as if I asked them how their day was, and they answered "purple". What does one have to do with the other?

In my mind, the question is if you want to do something, not whether you're already good at it. Why limit yourself to doing things you're already good at? Why limit your life to your comfort zone?

Let's be clear. I am not a dancer. I'm the whitest woman you ever saw, tall and awkward in this hip hop class. I am shy, a perfectionist, and hate looking like a fool. But so what? Being uncomfortable won't kill me. I wanted to take this class, so I am. It *is* uncomfortable, but I still love it.

I read a study once that showed a different chemical response in the brains of shy people, compared to those who aren't shy. I can't change my brain chemistry, but I don't have to let it hold me back from what I want to do. Some say that courage is being afraid and moving forward anyways. I try to be as courageous as I can, within my risk averse, timid nature. This is why I spent three months alone in South America studying Spanish. The reason I stood in front of the large crowd at Mike's service to give his eulogy.

It's also the reason I ride motorcycles. For the first year after getting my endorsement (motorcycle license), I'd ride every couple weeks. Each time I'd climb on my bike, my anxiety level was about 8.5 out of 10. There were glimpses of it being fun, but really, these practice rides were like taking medicine – good for me but not really enjoyable. Plus, the nerves made it harder to control the bike. When you're that tense, everything is jerky.

Finally, I decided that enough was enough. I had to get over this fear so I gave myself a "28-Day Challenge" to ride every day for four weeks. It is embarrassing to describe how hard this was. I had difficulty sleeping because I'd wake in the middle of the night and know that I'd have to ride to work in the morning. In the afternoon, I'd get tense knowing that my evening commute was coming up. Most days, I'd arrive home sweaty and shaky, hearing my heartbeat inside my helmet. I was so stressed I had stomach problems every day for the first two weeks. But I didn't quit.

There were small signs of improvement, and by the end of the four weeks, the 28-Day Challenge had done what I'd hoped. I could throw a leg over the bike without debilitating anxiety. This wasn't the end of my battles with nerves, but it was a major turning point. From that point on, I've found more and more pleasure in the ride.

I am not a natural rider. I have fought hard for every scrap of skill I possess. Sought out classes, books, advice, and practiced, practiced, practiced. Of course, I wish it came easily. Since Mike's death, I've wished many times that I could channel his skills. Since I am riding for both of us now, wouldn't that be fair? But it doesn't work that way. I am still just myself, not somehow the sum of both of us.

Like the dance class, the question isn't whether I'm talented at riding. The question is whether I want to do it. I don't get to choose how easy it is or how skilled I am. The only choice to make is this: will I continue or quit?

I choose to ride.

CHAPTER 15

Endurance

April 8, 2013

Now, eight months after Mike's death, much of this stage of grief is about being able to endure. Multiple times per week, I find myself saying, "I don't want to do this anymore." At work, sometimes I want to quit...but not just the job. Everything. I want to quit my life.

But what's the alternative? I could quit everything – sell everything and move. That doesn't buy me anything though. I'd just be grieving somewhere else, surrounded by moving boxes and completely overwhelmed, doing it all on my own. It would make me miss him worse than ever, make me more alone than ever. What's the point?

This is where I feel stuck in the middle. I'm not in the shock of immediate grief. But I also don't see the hope at the end of the road yet. I have blind faith that someday, I'll look up and be happy that I'm alive. I'll have one of those moments of pure gratitude for life. But that seems like a misty fairy tale now. So unreal it should be filed under paranormal, or fantasy, or romance.

I have never felt this alone in my life. Surrounded by lovely, wonderful people living their full and happy lives. I feel like an outsider, floating along, occasionally brushing up against others. Many times I feel forgotten. A part of me wants to put out the call publicly, just say straight out on Facebook... "Don't forget about me. The hard part isn't over."

I admit it. I often think about what different people would say if I didn't make it through this. If I died somehow. The people who don't know me well would shake their heads at the tragedy of it. But the people who do know me well, the people who love me? They would never forgive me, and they would never forgive themselves. I could not do that to them. So yet again, I am protecting other people.

Part of me says to them, "I am trapped in this hell for you. So that you don't spend the rest of your life wishing you had reached out more. So please...reach out more."

I know that I'm difficult to be around these days. I can be negative, sometimes snippy. I talk about things that normal people don't talk about - burials and the like. Sometimes I'm a party pooper and have sad moments, often when surrounded by crowds of happy people.

I can be difficult to reach or to make plans with. Mentally, I'm still not entirely recovered. Sometimes I lose focus. I have bad habits of compulsively checking for messages then losing track of them.

But please, don't forget about me. Don't be put off by the above. Reach out and reach out and keep reaching out. It matters. It helps me want to endure another day, then another, then another...until someday, I will look up with gratitude, happy to be alive.

Postscript...

I want to be clear that I am not going to kill myself. These are just the thoughts that go through my head. In my grief class, the facilitator said that this is very normal. Most of us in grief have moments where we feel that ceasing to exist would be the easier path.

I have vacillated over whether to share this post. It seems too raw. It might worry people. But in the first post of my blog, I stated that this is the place where I can be honest. Where I don't have to protect the people around me. Where I don't have to censor myself. Suicide is a taboo topic. In my mind, this taboo makes it even more important to be open about it.

I hope people in grief will read my story and recognize parts of it in their own journey. Maybe it will help them feel less alone. I hope that people who haven't experienced grief yet will find pieces they can relate to and parts that are surprising. Maybe they will take something away that will help them be a good companion to someone in grief. A watered down, censored version of this blog would not be good for anyone, myself included.

CHAPTER 16

The dog trial

April 11, 2013

Mike and I had been planning on getting a dog when he returned from this last deployment. After his death, I was unsure whether to move ahead with this plan. On the downside: I've never had a dog and don't know the ins-and-outs of being a good dog owner or training a dog. I travel a lot for work. And my biggest concern: would I be trapped at home, unable to leave the dog for all-day rides, full days in Seattle, etc.? There's also the niggling doubt raised by the fact that you're not supposed to make any big life decisions in the first few years after a loss.

On the positive side: The dog would provide love and companionship. A couple of weeks after the accident, I was texting with Mike's sister. She asked if I was still planning on getting a dog, and I replied, "Yes. I need someone to love in the house." On a walk with a friend, I confessed that I wanted a dog because I was afraid that I'd get so lonely that I'd make bad decisions. What if I slept with someone out of sheer loneliness? In those early days of shock, this seemed like a real possibility. (It hasn't happened.)

After the service in September, I spent hours searching the Petfinder website. It was akin to using an online dating site. Look at the picture; is he/she attractive? Read the stats and bio. Are we compatible? Do we have similar interests and lifestyles? I'd stare at the dog profiles and think, "Are you the one for me?"

Finally, one night I found her: Madeline, a nine-month-old lab mix, described as friendly and gentle. I contacted the rescue organization, and they sent me the application. As a non-dog owner, I was surprised by the extensive application process. In addition to the long form, they requested photos of the house and yard, copies of a utility bill, two references, and a note from the landlord. I quickly assembled all of it.

The application form was interesting:

Why do you want a dog? "My boyfriend died in a motorcycle accident in August. I need a loving companion for my home."

Number of adults and children in the home? "One" *[Ugh. Only one.]*

What will happen to your animal(s) in the event of an unexpected medical emergency with you? "Friends would help." *[Crossing my fingers here. Since my backup is gone, I need to rely on friends…]*

Why do you think you would be a good dog owner? "I am responsible and loving." *[How the heck should I know? Maybe I won't be a good dog owner.]*

A few days after turning in the application, I heard that Madeline had been adopted by a nice couple. This news made me cry. I just had to trust that the right dog was out there. Over the next several months, finding a dog was put on the back-burner due to lots of work travel. Also, I still wasn't 100% sure that getting a dog was the right move.

A few weeks ago, a friend asked if I could pet sit for her Pomeranian mix. Perfect! A dog trial. Maybe this would answer my questions about whether a dog is right for me. I picked Frankie up on Thursday and had her through Sunday afternoon.

This was the first time I had ever taken care of a dog. We went on at least two walks per day. We played keep-away with her stuffed bunny as I chased her around the coffee table. I smuggled her into work. We ran a 5k together. She slept curled on the bed.

So...the verdict? Having a dog was less of a hassle than I expected but also less comforting. On the positive side: Frankie was easy to care for and good company. On the negative side: Since Mike's death, I have missed physical touch. Cuddling with the right person allows all the tension to flow away. I hoped that snuggling with a lap dog would provide this connection and comfort, but it didn't.

In the middle of the night when my breath caught with grief, I reached out for Frankie. She immediately turned to let me rub her belly. She enjoyed it, and it felt good to me too, but my breathing did not ease. I did not feel less alone. She provided companionship but not ease for my heart. Maybe that is too much to ask of any dog.

I also found that caring for Frankie created a subtle pressure to be home or to choose activities where she could come along. Spending too much time alone makes me depressed, even when I have a dog.

For now, it's not the right time for a dog.

Frankie

CHAPTER 17

Disappearing

April 12, 2013

Since the burial, my longing for Mike physically has dissipated. This is a gift, not to be tormented by something that felt so close, yet I could never have again. His body, his touch, his hug, his kiss.

But the flip side of the coin is...it feels as if he's disappearing. Looking at photos of him last night, I stopped at a self-portrait of us. It was snapped while hiking the Hoh rainforest in February 2012. I'm leaning back against his chest and holding the camera high. His eyes are the best part of the photo - soft and warm and happy. He looks straight through the lens and melts my heart.

I almost don't remember the feeling of leaning back and resting my head against his chest. I remember doing it but not the feeling of it. It's misty and distant. This makes me feel disloyal. It scares me. I don't want to let him go.

CHAPTER 18

Facts (month one)

April 17, 2013

In the early days after the accident, I can't tell you how many times I heard the words, "I can't imagine." Friend after friend came up, expressed their condolences, then said, "I can't imagine what you're going through." Perhaps in response to this litany, I started a list on my phone, entitled Facts. It contains snippets that describe my experience in the first month after the accident. I'm not sure why it's called Facts, except that when I was so completely unmoored, it was amusing to think that anything was as immutable as a fact. Read as a group, the headings are humorous and heartbreaking all at once.

To place this list in context, my overriding memory from the first month is feeling like a cornhusk vibrating: an empty, dry, fragile shell, shaking in rhythm with the oscillations of a keening wail that only I could hear. A cloud of panic floated over my shoulder, ready to descend with a moment's relaxation of vigilance. I had to be careful not to think too much and, most especially, not to think of the future. That would invite the panic to descend.

Here are the "facts" from month one. The headings are the list from my phone, drafted in that first month. I've added explanations for you here.

- **I don't like voicemail.** There are two voicemails from Mike saved on my cell. Every three weeks, Verizon makes me re-save them before they'll let me listen to a new message. It takes me days to work up the nerve to listen to a new message because I might have to listen to Mike's voice first.

- **Auto-fill is the devil.** I texted a number of people the day after the accident. Now, when I enter the words "my boyfriend" into a text, the next word suggested is "died". Similarly, when I type "how are you today," the next word it prompts is "baby".

- **Turning the calendar is hard.** While Mike was on deployment, turning the calendar was a big deal. It meant he was an entire month closer to coming home. We were another third of the way through the deployment. After the accident, it felt like I had wished him home so strongly that he slingshot past me. How could the calendar turn to September without him here? I couldn't bear to turn the calendars and made my friends do it.

- **Any sentence beginning with "at least" isn't anything I want to hear right now. Other inauspicious beginnings include, "not to downplay your situation but".** Sometimes when talking with my friends I'd share something difficult about the situation. In their need to make it all better, they'd try to look at the bright side. For example, I said to a friend, "I can't believe he died the day after returning." My friend's response: "At least you had that last night with him. Just think of all the Army widows who didn't have that last night, whose husbands died on deployment." Then I felt guilty for complaining about my situation and shut down to sharing anything further. Another friend tried to comfort me by sharing his sister's loss: "Not to downplay your situation, but my sister lost her husband, and they were married 23 years." Comparing griefs is not productive - or possible.

- **I am self-conscious about my hair loss.** I lost one-third to one-half of my hair in the first month.
- **None of my clothes fit right, unless they have spandex.** Despite forcing myself to eat, I dropped 10 lbs in the first two weeks. At 5'10", my size four dress was baggy at the service. I didn't recognize myself in the mirror. It felt like a sham to leave my Facebook profile photo up because I looked nothing like it. You could see that the light had left my spirit.
- **It's possible to do pretty much anything while crying: eat, drive, order a beer.** I did all of these in the first month. There wasn't any use waiting for the tears to pass, like a rain squall. They were so unpredictable, it was better to push through.
- **My Facebook posts are honest, but only the vaguely hopeful items end up there.**
- **I am tired of doing hard things.**
- **I don't understand the advantage of being strong.** I can't tell you how many people told me that I was strong. They said it in admiring tones, as a compliment. They said that my strength was inspiring. It made me want to scream. In my mind, strength is choosing to walk the hard path. I did not choose this. If there was any place in the world I could go where this was not real, I would be

there. I am craven, not courageous. Yes, I get up every day and put one foot in front of the other, but that is because there is no choice. Or, there is no choice that would make it better. The word of the day recently was "polylemma: a choice involving multiple undesirable options." It describes this situation perfectly. When there are no desirable options, you pick the only option that makes sense and keep moving forward.

- **I am afraid of how my friendships might change with my friends in couples.** Several of my divorced friends told me that all their friends in couples dropped them when they became single. They no longer fit in, and they were seen as threatening. I was afraid my friends would disappear.

- **Certain social situations give me claustrophobia now.** Anything like a party, or a class, or a church service – anywhere I couldn't break down without causing a scene – made me feel trapped and panicky.

- **"Beloved" describes who I lost. Not boyfriend, partner, or significant other.**

- **Very mixed feelings about personal grooming.** In preparation for Mike's return from deployment, I got my hair cut and my nails done. I plucked, shaved, waxed, and picked my clothes with care. I had a deep aversion to doing any of this after he died. It was hard to accept that my body was continuing on when I felt that everything about me had stopped when he died.

- **The moments when I feel normal or good, I feel guilty.**

- **The nightmare.** Described in the "Non-PC confessions" post.

- **Very mixed feelings about the Navy.** Described in the "Just the girlfriend" post.
- **No kids.** Walking to work my first day back, I saw a woman ahead pushing a stroller. Suddenly, it hit me that I probably won't ever have kids. I started sobbing and had to sit on a bench until it passed. Mike and I hadn't entirely decided if we were going to have kids together, though it was becoming less likely as we got older. But now, that option is gone. For a fleeting, selfish moment, I wished that I was pregnant, as a way to hold on to him, a way for part of him to live on.
- **I am not jealous of other couples. I don't want what they have. I want what we had.**
- **Saying goodbye to Mike's bikes will be hard.** I dreaded selling his bikes. And it was just as hard as I feared. I cried harder after the bikes rode off than at any point prior, including the service. I was still waiting for someone to tell me that it was all a mistake, that the accident hadn't happened. But he never would have sold all his bikes if he was still here. The sound of his bikes starting up and riding away opened my heart and ripped it out all at once.
- **My crazy year.** A friend who lost her husband to a stroke told me that she had thought she was normal during the first year after his death, but looking back, she wasn't. She was crazy. I've decided that this is my crazy year, and I don't need to feel any pressure to act normal.
- **I am more myself than I've ever been. I don't have the energy to try to be what you want me to be.** One sign of this is in my writing. I used to avoid using "big words" because I didn't want to look snooty. But it takes

too much energy to filter everything that I say and translate it into more common words. Since the accident, I have decided that if it's in my heart, it's coming out in the same form. No translating.

- **Every individual piece of this is the hardest thing I've ever done.**

CHAPTER 19

Just the girlfriend

April 20, 2013

Part One: Definitions

When you're in a solid relationship, there's no need to explain it to anyone. It oozes out of you when you're together. It's completely obvious to all around you. It's a fact. Indisputable. This is how it was for Mike and me. We weren't married, but it didn't matter. We knew what we had, and that's all that mattered. Until he died...

Suddenly, the word "boyfriend" was grossly inadequate. I found myself explaining our relationship to strangers. "My boyfriend died in a motorcycle accident," I'd say, followed by, "It was a serious relationship" or "We lived together." It sounded vaguely desperate.

Oddly, I wasn't the only one who struggled with this. People around me tried different terms, phrases and explanations. Mike's parents wrote me into the obituary as his "longtime girlfriend". My mom alternately used the terms "partner" and "significant other".

All these phrases fell short. I found myself wishing that we had been married simply so that I could say "my husband died", and people would understand the magnitude of my grief.

It wasn't until a month after the accident that I found the right term to describe who had died. At the first meeting of my grief class, the facilitator started the orientation with, "Some of you lost a parent. Some of you lost a child. Some of you lost your beloved." "That's it!" I crowed silently. "That's who I lost. My beloved."

I never would have introduced him as "my beloved" when he was alive, and I haven't done so since he died, but it's comforting to have that word tucked away in my heart.

Part Two: Proof

After the accident, I found myself trying to justify my role in Mike's life, trying to prove that what we had was real, despite the fact that I was "only a girlfriend". In multiple conversations, our friends kept telling me, "We know that you and Mike were practically married." In my heart and in the eyes of everyone who knew us well, I mattered. I was the most important person in Mike's daily life, as he was in mine.

But in the eyes of any official organization, I not only wasn't important, *I did not exist.* At the burial in March, Mike's parents shared the scrapbook that they've assembled since he died. Page after page of letters of condolence from the Navy, the organ donation agencies, even the President of the United States. Mike's son has a similar collection in his "Daddy's book". I have none of those.

I would not trade places with them, his parents or son. Unfortunately, they lived far away from us. To them, those letters must seem a cold comfort when they consider the time apart since he was stationed in Washington. But still, seeing the letters collected like that...it makes me feel lesser. It makes me feel invisible.

In life, I could not have mattered more. He prioritized me above most everything. But in death, there is no place for me.

Part Three: The Navy

I feel deeply ambivalent about the Navy. The guys on the boat could not have treated me with more sensitivity and respect at every step of the way. These men gave up their vacations to plan the service. One postponed his transfer to help. They delivered flowers to the house; performed the most beautiful and moving service; sat with me the entire time the movers packed up his stuff. They offered to help with any repairs to the house or anything else that I needed from then on. They looked at me with concern, and fear, and solemnity, and respect, and sensitivity. They looked like they wanted to rip out their own hearts, wracking their brains to think of any tiny scrap of help or comfort they could give me. I cannot fault them in any way for their treatment.

But you have to understand. Mike had nothing to do with the Navy in his off time. I knew no one from the boat before the accident. We had never attended a social event with the boat. I didn't know any of the wives and wasn't on any "phone trees" to get news of the boat when they were out to sea. I hadn't even seen him in his uniform until we moved in together. The Navy was something completely outside of my life.

Then he died, and the Navy landed on me. It flattened me. In one fell swoop with Mike's death, I became a guest in my own life. The Navy stepped in and took over. They came into my home and went through our possessions. They planned the memorial service, including setting the date. Because we were not married, I had no official standing.

Only through the grace of others was I gifted the most deeply held and personal portions of my life. Only through the grace of his family was I able to join them in the side room before the service, sit with them during the service, and deliver a eulogy. Only through the grace of his family was I able to keep any of our joint possessions that made our home feel like a home. Only through the grace of the master chief and other guys from the boat was I able to keep my self-respect as the process moved forward, as the "Big Navy" steamrolled my life.

Mike's parents were absolutely, amazingly lovely to me. They told me to keep anything that had sentimental value. The difficulty was deciding what had sentimental value. I'd pick up some mundane, everyday item and think, "Am I going to regret not having this in a month? In a year? Would it be more meaningful to his dad? To his son?" What awful decisions. In the shock of immediate grief, there's no way to answer those questions.

Thank God I was on the lease, and his parents liked me. Without these two godsends, the Navy could have put me on the front porch and emptied out the entire house. There would have been no way to prove what was mine. I shudder at the thought. Not at the loss of "stuff" but at the violation. I am grateful. I think in horror about how much worse it could have been. But still, when I think of the Navy, that whole sequence of events, my chest tightens.

(We lived in a private house in town, not in Navy housing. Still, the Navy had the right – and obligation – to enter the house and pack and ship his personal goods, everything he owned, to his next of kin, his parents.)

One day in my grief class, one of the ladies arrived distraught. It turned out that her family had gone against her wishes and opened the storage unit with her loved one's belongings. She said, "It's only been five months since he died! I'm not ready." We all reassured her that she had the right to set those boundaries with her family.

In my heart though, I felt a deep jealousy. Five months? What a luxury. I had five *weeks* to go through Mike's stuff before they packed it up and took it away. To tell the truth, I couldn't face it until the night before the inventory. A friend sat with me as I frantically made one decision after another, trying to move too fast to feel anything. *I* was not ready.

This experience has changed me. When Mike was alive, I used to think, "We know what we have. Why get married?" Now, I think, "Why not?" If you have the emotional side and the commitment, why not have the legal protections too? Why not be more than "just the girlfriend"?

Postscript…

After drafting this post, I realized that even *I* had been suckered into the false connotations of the word "girlfriend". I've been feeling lately like maybe I should be healing faster. It wasn't until writing the words "my husband died" above that I realized that if he had been my husband, I wouldn't feel any such pressure. No one would expect a widow to heal in eight months from the unexpected loss of a husband.

CHAPTER 20

Kinky crafts

April 23, 2013

On Sunday, a small group of girlfriends held a bachelorette for a girlfriend. I had planned the day, and luckily, it went really well. All four of us were motorcycle riders. I had met the bride because her fiancé rode with Mike.

The day started with a funny craft project. A local sex shop was holding an Earth Day Kinky Crafts Workshop, where they taught how to make floggers out of recycled bicycle tire inner tubes. I thought it would be random, funny, and fun. So...there we were, four women ranging from mid-30's to late-40's, standing in a cheery, brightly painted sex shop run by women.

The workshop began with a 15-minute presentation on how to incorporate spanking into bedroom play. The presenter discussed the importance of communication and safety, a few different techniques, and the sensations that different materials could produce. As she talked, I was caught off-guard by a "grief-burst". My eyes slid across the walls searching for distraction as I sniffled and tried not to cry. Hearing her matter-of-fact descriptions of sex brought to mind so vividly the intimate part of our relationship.

Unlike other parts of the grief process, this loss is one that I haven't faced head-on. In fact, I've tried not to think of it at all. I haven't come to terms with the fact that we will never share that intimacy again. And I haven't come to terms with the future. It's equally horrifying that I might be alone forever as that I might not be. I'm not ready to deal with this yet so I put it aside.

After creating our floggers, we walked down to a bakery. Along the way, we talked about where the bride and groom might live. He's in the military so they have some choices coming up. She is part owner of a business so they have been living apart for several months as she wrapped up a busy season of work. She said that they both didn't care where they ended up, as long as they were together. They were tired of living apart.

"Amen," I said silently in my heart. If you do not need to be apart, don't. Actively choose to be with the people you love. Don't sit idly by, letting life carry you along, letting the urgencies of work or logistics drive your decisions. Stand up and vote with your feet, let your actions in every way demonstrate your priorities. And let those priorities be around spending time with those you love.

I do not have any regrets in this area. Mike and I absolutely prioritized our time together. We made sure to get our work done during work hours so our free time could be spent together. I worked my ass off before he'd get home from deployment so I could take time off with him when he returned. Because our time together was so limited by his deployments, it could not have been more precious.

No, I do not have regrets, but I do have sadness for the future plans we never had a chance to complete, for the opportunities that have come up since his death that he would have loved. Silently, in my heart I told the bride, "Don't look at your life together stretching before you and think that you have all the time in the world. If it is truly important, do it now. The future is unknown."

After the bakery and a stroll through the outdoor sculpture park, we went to an Italian restaurant. As we settled into the bar, I turned around to see the bride backlit with the sun shining through the windows. "You're so beautiful," I told her. "Really? I feel like I'm getting a little long in the tooth," she replied. "We will all get old," I choked out before the tears caught up with me. This time there was no holding them back. "But if you are a beautiful person, you will always be beautiful."

At the end of the evening, we hugged and bid each other goodbye then turned to step out on our separate paths in life. She began her cross-country drive back to her fiancé's arms. And I boarded the ferry and floated home through the darkness.

CHAPTER 21

Food for the soul

May 3, 2013

Today, a discussion on the motorcycle forum surprised me. It touched me. Someone posted about an accident they saw. When another rider asked the purpose of "rider down" threads, this was the response:

> *It serves to inform a segment of the community that one of their own may need support. Those that have the time and/or means can then step up and provide some assistance and relief to the rider and family during the rough time ahead.*
>
> *I have seen threads similar to this that have resulted in funds being raised to help support a family during recovery. I've also seen how something simple like a brother/sister picking up the wrecked bike from the police lot keeping serious hunger off the doorstep.*
>
> *If nothing else, it gives you a chance to show compassion to another human being by expressing empathy and hope. Even something as simple as that can make the difference in recovering quickly or not at all.*
>
> *So when you ask what purpose does a thread like this serve, I have to answer it serves to provide food for the soul of everyone: you, me, the*

person(s) in need and everyone else that would do the same if you were the downed rider.

I have no idea if every accident should be posted or not, but I do have something to say about the comments that are posted in the "rider down" threads.

The accident may be minor, serious, or fatal. We may never know. But if someone finds a newspaper article and posts it, then the rider's name will be connected to the thread. Quite likely, the rider or their family will eventually Google and find the conversation.

When Mike died, every compassionate comment in his RIP thread was food for the soul. Regardless of whether the poster knew Mike or not, the respect and sentiment expressed mattered. It mattered to me and also to his family. They read everything posted there and were touched more than you know. Thank you. Thank you.

Since then, I have tried to reach out and support others in need, to give back to the community that has given me so much. This is food for my soul too.

In February, a coworker mentioned that she had commented in one of the funeral home websites for Mike. That evening, I decided to search for it. Doing a Google search under his name also brought up the newspaper articles about the accident, with the comments. The comments saying that he deserved to die...for riding a sport bike, for whatever assumption the reader had made about him...well, those hit home too.

I thought I was okay until I realized that it was 10:30 pm; the heater had gone off a half hour prior, meaning that it was 65 degrees in the house; and I was flushed and sweating. Seriously sweating, like through my sweats and lap blanket, the back of the keyboard was covered with condensation. I was not okay.

We have a choice in the words we put out into the world, if we want to feed the soul or wither it. Words have power. I vote for feeding the soul, for lifting people up, for doing what I can to ensure that another grieving person isn't sitting alone in the dark winter, reading the message that their loved one deserved to die.

CHAPTER 22

Companioning

May 5, 2013

A couple nights ago, I finally realized that it doesn't matter how much my friends reach out. They could smother me with attention, and I would still feel alone, still *be* alone. There is no replacement for Mike. My frustration with them melted away. I released it.

What it comes down to is...I not only lost my life partner, I lost my best friend. I lost the person I would have leaned on to get through this difficult journey. For example, after I got the news that Mike had died, I just sat there. I knew I should call someone but couldn't figure out who. The only person who came to mind was Mike.

I know that it's not possible to compare griefs, but in the deep down corner of my heart, almost unacknowledged, I am jealous of people who are mourning a different relationship. If they still have someone to lean on...boy, that would be nice.

Of course, their losses are difficult in different ways. It's a specious argument since every loss is a uniquity. While there are some universalities to the experience, at the end of the day, grief is a solitary journey. No one can travel the path for you. Even if you have a companion by your side, you still walk alone.

That said, I need to remember not to give up on reaching out, on connecting with the world, with humanity. The book from my grief class calls it companioning people on their grief journeys. The book stresses over and over how important it is to find people who welcome your stories, who will listen to you and companion you. I need to prioritize ways to include this in my daily life.

The trick is finding people who really want to hear it, as opposed to people who patiently listen but would really rather be somewhere else. Grief is a strange and twisty journey. It's surprising in so many ways, both in unexpected gifts and heartbreaks. I need to find people who want to accompany me as I discover the way, step by step.

CHAPTER 23

The secret in my pocket

May 11, 2013

You may be wondering when we'll get to the "hope" part of this blog on grief, hope, and motorcycles. Well, here is a post about hope. I will share a secret with you.

My first day back to work after the accident was Monday, September 17th. On that day, I walked my normal route, scared and lost and hopeless. Lost in almost every sense of the word. And most certainly hopeless. Truthfully, I hadn't yet decided if I wanted to live. I found it easier to say, "He is dead," than "I am alive."

In that timeframe, I often wished that I had died with him or instead of him. As I went through the days after the accident, I imagined how he would have handled each step if he had been the survivor. He was my ghostly companion. In the still of the night, I would whisper to him in a small voice, "You should be here instead. You would be better at this than me."

On that first day back to work, if you had asked if I had hope, I would have looked at you with bleak eyes and mute lips.

And yet....and yet.... I stopped on that walk to scoop up an acorn. The humble acorn, pregnant with the dormant DNA map for a mighty tree. Needing only the right conditions, this acorn will grow and change, set strong roots deeply into the earth, and reach, reach, reach for the sky.

This simple act was an act of hope. Even in my days of mute yearning, when I could not utter the word "hope", something in me reached out and picked it up. For months now, the acorn has secretly lived in my jacket pocket. I finger it when I need comfort or want to calm my anxiety. It is precious. Each time I remove something from my pocket, I carefully hold the acorn to make sure it doesn't fall out. It is my hope, and I don't want to lose it.

This acorn is not ready to become a tree yet, just as I am not ready to step forth as my new self yet. Until that day, I hold my secret hope in my pocket. It is my talisman, rubbed smooth with time, with connection, with love. It is my companion on this journey, both of us awaiting the day when we will be set free to follow our destiny, to seek the sun, to reach for the sky.

Humble acorn. My hope.

CHAPTER 24

Mother's Day

This is a post of musings and memories about mothers and Mother's Day.

Part One

May 12, 2013

Today is Mother's Day. A day loaded with meaning, with expectation, with memories. I am spending it in Hawaii with my mom. This trip is a long time coming. Mom was in the process of moving to Hawaii when the accident happened. Her condo was sold; her stuff was in storage; and she was at an extended-stay hotel for the final few weeks. After the accident, she canceled her plans and rented a house seven minutes away from mine, just to make sure she was close when I needed her. My mom is amazing.

Since the accident, she has invited me to Hawaii at least four times, and I have declined. While grateful for the offer, I just couldn't face it. The last time I was in Hawaii was December of 2011. This was a long-planned family vacation with my mom and brother. At the tail end of the trip, Mike's sub pulled into Oahu for a port call. It was pure coincidence that we were in

Hawaii at the same time. We both leapt into action. I booked an inter-island flight from Maui to Oahu and changed my return flight. He quickly booked a room at the Hale Koa (military hotel in Waikiki) and a car. Even though he still had to work, those three days were bliss. He had been out to sea for about a month so the time together was sweet and precious.

I was even able to take him out for his 35th birthday, which fell in those three days. We went to a Japanese restaurant, Nobu, where I splurged on the most expensive chef's tasting menus available. It was an amazing meal with eye-opening flavors, a completely new experience for us. With tip, that meal cost over $400, easily three times more than any meal I had ever purchased. I knew that I should have felt guilt at spending that money on a fleeting experience, but I didn't. I felt pure contentment. It was an astonishing, almost transformative meal, well worth sharing with the man I loved, on his 35th birthday, in a tropical locale that we had not expected to visit together. What a precious, pure memory. Thinking back on it now, I have no regrets...only gratitude.

But it was these powerful, emotionally charged memories that made me afraid to return to Hawaii. I was afraid that it would feel like I was traveling towards him. I was afraid it would make me yearn for him, that it would make him feel close yet unattainable.

So...why am I here now? The short answer is "Mother's Day". The latest invitation to Hawaii came this spring. Mom had made plans to be there May 1-15, ostensibly for her birthday, but mainly to escape the dreary Pacific Northwest skies. As we sat on her couch after Easter brunch, I said tentatively that I was thinking about taking her up on her invitation but only for one week. My desire for a "Monet moment" (see prior post) had been growing, and possibly a week in Hawaii would fulfill it. She smiled and said that it would be great not to spend Mother's Day alone. That sealed the deal. There was no going back, no way I could say no after that.

I decided to view this trip as a trial. One of the interesting parts of grief is that you never know what will be difficult and what won't. Sometimes the things you dread end up being easy...and sometimes not. But you don't know until you are there. While the flight out was difficult, so far, being here has been okay emotionally.

Yesterday, we went on a snorkeling trip. There were 25 of us on the boat, including a Brazilian family: mother, father, six-year-old girl, and 18-month-old boy. He had cherubic cheeks and a bright smile as he explored the dock before we boarded. An hour into the boat ride, he started crying, and the father gathered him in his arms and held the soft weight of him as he quieted and slept for at least an hour.

I watched this father and son and couldn't help thinking that Mike's parents had once done the same for him. They had held and loved and comforted him. He was a Christmas baby, and his mom tells of nursing him by the light of the Christmas tree.

Watching this father hold his son on the boat, the thought crossed my mind: "Will you grow up to die at 35 too? Will your parents love you and care for you and shepherd you into adulthood, only to have you throw yourself off a desert road?" Immediately after thinking it, I felt like a horrid person. Who looks at a sweet tableau of parental love and thinks of death? Apparently, I do.

One of the hardest parts of losing Mike is imagining how it must be for his parents losing a son – and his son losing a father. Mike was the only boy amidst three sisters. There are some dates

I watch approach with fear because I expect that they will be painful for his family. Mother's Day is one of those dates.

I ordered flowers to be sent to Mike's mom today. He used to send her flowers on Mother's Day, and if there is anything I could do to ease her loss today, to fill the void, I wanted to try. I sent her a text message this morning: "Happy Mother's Day, Mom! I know that today can't be easy. Sending you bunches of hugs and love." She quickly replied. "Thank you. Only ¾ here but will gladly take you for the other ¼. Love you and love the flowers. Hope you and mom have a special day." Since the accident, Mike's mom has gathered me into her arms and taken me as one of her own. She is one of the blessings that have come out of the accident. I hope that seeing me as family helps to heal and comfort her as well.

I also texted Mike's son's mom (Mike's ex-wife) and wished her a happy Mother's Day. Her reply also surprised and touched me: "Thank you. Happy day to celebrate you for being such a great influence and loving and supporting Chris. You are such a blessing. Thank you."

Even though I am not a mom and probably won't ever be one, I can have a role in loving this special young man. That is what I heard in her message. She is not threatened by my love for him but welcomes it. As two grieving souls, there is something that he and I can give each other that no one else can. It is a special connection. I treasure him.

Part Two

May 13, 2013

Mother's Day is also significant in a different way. Last year, Mother's Day was the day Mike left for deployment. When he returned three and a half months later, I picked him up at the airport, and we drove south to meet his friends to go on the long-awaited motorcycle trip. He never made it home. It is now one year since he was home, in our home.

It is an anniversary of sorts, though of course, not a happy one. Maybe it is odd that I have been tracking this date. After the accident, time felt strangely disjointed. He had only been dead for X *weeks*, but he had been gone from our home for X *months*. As time passed since the accident, I have been counting towards the one-year mark of the accident and also the one-year mark of him leaving our home. This anniversary was heavy in my thoughts today.

You never know where you will come upon comfort and recognition of grief. This morning mom and I attended a timeshare presentation. Near the end, the saleslady stepped away. I quickly checked email and found that the next session of the grief class is starting in June. Mom and I were talking about it when the saleslady returned. She overheard and asked if she could give me a hug.

I have become a connoisseur of hugs since the accident, and this wasn't a simple, polite hug. No, this was a down-deep heart hug that lasted at least 20 seconds. As she released me, she whispered in my hair that she had lost her son. He had died in a drunk driving accident. This hug was not only a comfort for me but also for this grieving mother.

And a final story to recount about mothers: This trip has been good for me and my mom. There has been a distance between us since the accident. Last week, I had a nightmare that both my parents died, that I was almost alone in the world. This dream has been living in the back of my thoughts. I don't want to have any regrets so tonight I grasped an opportunity to draw us closer.

After dinner, we carried some homemade macaroons out to the picnic tables by the ocean. There is an intimacy created by sitting in the moonlight by the waves and the sand in the humid, salty air. We opened the treats, and I asked if she would like to hear some of my writing. I read her the post, "On riding two-up", my voice rising over the soft crash of the waves. She answered with a smile and, "That is beautiful." Next, I read the entry, "Kinky crafts". I looked up to find her sobbing, head and shoulders bowed under the weight of grief, all of her strength drained away. I reached out, touched her arm, and simply gave her space to deal with the storm.

This opened us to discussing why we don't talk about Mike. I shared with her that there are two reasons I don't lean on her more. First, she wants *so badly* to make it better. It's overwhelming. I don't need someone to make it better, to leap into action, to jump up and save me. I need someone to accompany me. Someone to listen with all of their soul present. Not thinking about how they can fix it. Not thinking about another story triggered by mine. Not rushing to grab tissues or to hug me. Simply being absolutely present with 100% of their being. Creating a sacred space for the stories, by the power of being a witness.

The other reason I don't lean on her more? She has barely started to deal with his loss herself. The things that I have to say make the loss so real for her that it throws her off balance. It makes her hurt, and I hate to do that. I recommended (again) that she take the grief class, and I think that she will now. I am glad. I think it will help us grow together. She is my mom, and I love her.

CHAPTER 25

Forgiveness

May 17, 2013

Ah yes, forgiveness, we finally come to you. This is a topic I've been avoiding, but I can only avert my eyes for so long.

This is the elephant in the room. Let's face it, shall we? Let's talk about guilt, blame, fault, fate, and yes, forgiveness.

Since the hours immediately after the accident, I have known that it was my fault. I did not operate the bike, did not throw him off the road. But yet...**he would not have been there if not for me.**

It was my idea to pick him up at the airport with the bike loaded in the truck. It started as a joke. We laughed about the looks he would get from the other guys on the boat. As his return date slipped further and further back, this joke transitioned into reality. It was the only way that he would be able to join his friends on part of their annual road trip.

I was happy to make it happen because I knew how much he looked forward to this trip every year. I packed his gear and supplies and handled all the logistics. I arranged for one of his friends to look over the bike to make sure it was ready. Another friend helped load the bike in the back of the truck. On a Tuesday morning, I drove it to the airport to pick him up and deliver him to his demise.

We did everything we could to make sure he would be okay. I wouldn't let him drive on the way to Baker City so that he could rest. He decided not to have even one drink the night before the accident, though he had gone without for the length of the deployment. We went to sleep at 10:00 pm so he could get a full night's rest. His bike was in tip top shape. He wore full leather gear. He said that he would stay at the back of the group for the first half of the day to warm up.

The plan seemed reasonable. He was a very experienced rider, with well-functioning equipment, riding with three of his favorite riding buddies. They had ridden so many miles together that they were almost extensions of each others' thoughts. As I kissed him goodbye and took the final photo, I had no premonitions.

Looking back now, this plan was A Very Bad Idea, for many reasons. Here are the top three:

1) Usually, when he returned from deployment, his sub pulled into Guam about a week before he flew home. He would have a week to acclimate and rest up. This time was different. They did not return until the day before the flight. He had duty so rather than get a couple hours of sleep then get up and head to the airport, he stayed awake. He didn't sleep well on the flights, and he slept very little on the drive down to Baker City. At dinner on Tuesday night in Baker City, he mentioned that he had been up for about 60 hours.

2) Another factor was his eyes. Because there was so little time between when the sub pulled in and when they flew out of Guam, his eyes didn't have time to adjust. The Navy says that

the sailors shouldn't operate motor vehicles for 24 hours after returning because their depth perception is skewed from having lived for months in an environment with limited space, where they cannot focus on anything far away. I didn't know this before the accident. The master chief explained it to me while the movers packed Mike's stuff to return to his family.

3) It was a bad idea to take someone who hadn't touched a bike in over three months and drop him with three riders who were several days into a road trip. These riders were at the top of their game, and Mike wasn't. (I do not blame his friends *at all*.)

Of course, there are a million tiny decisions that one could say led to the accident, but I say that most of them would have been moot if **he wasn't there**.

If I had asked him to stay with me upon his return, said a single word in that direction, he would have dropped the road trip in a heartbeat. He always placed me first. But this is an interesting point...because I cannot think of any permutation of our relationship where I would have asked for that. Just as he placed me first, I did so for him.

I did everything I could to help him do whatever made him happy. On two prior road trips, I drove all night to help when he was stranded with mechanical issues. On one of those trips, I delivered a fresh bike so he could continue on the trip. While I dearly wish I had asked him to stay with me this time, I cannot imagine having done so in the context of our relationship, for anything other than safety concerns. And when we made this plan, we didn't know how late the sub would be getting in. I didn't fully understand the risks.

So...this brings us to fate: the question of whether the accident was fated to happen. If changing any small decision on the way to that accident scene would have avoided it. Or if this accident was the fated end to his life, in which case, all possible choices would have led to the same ending. If I believe in fate, then the accident is not my responsibility. If not, then it is my fault, at least in part.

Last week in Hawaii, I had a reading from a psychic. I don't know if I believe in psychics, but I was open to giving it a shot. The first card she pulled was Forgiveness. I smiled ruefully. My friends - guilt, blame, fault - I knew that I would not be able to avoid them forever. Forgiveness is just the opposite side of these coins.

Do I forgive myself? I don't know. I do think that actions have consequences, and my actions here definitely did. I put him in a bad situation. There is no getting around that fact. But I also cannot imagine making a different choice, in the context of our relationship, with the information we had at the time. And I don't know if I believe in fate. Sometimes yes and sometimes no.

What does this all add up to? An uneasy equilibrium. I wish it wrapped up in a nice bow, but I'm just not there yet. It's an evolution, and I'm not done evolving. We'll revisit Forgiveness in a couple months.

CHAPTER 26

Memorial Day

May 30, 2013

Last weekend was Memorial Day. It ambushed me, sideswiped me with a storm of emotion. Several threads were posted on the motorcycle forums honoring service members. Two of them included photos of grieving women in military cemeteries.

The first was a young woman lying on the grass with her head bowed, in bare feet and a sundress, water bottle by her side, like a picnic gone wrong. I felt such a kinship with her. I could feel the band of the sundress cutting across my back as if I were wearing it. I looked at how it fell across her body and thought, "No, the hips should be a little bigger, more curve to her bum," as if her body should be mine. As if I should be inhabiting the photo.

But the photo that truly hit home, that propelled the storm of tears, was the second one. This was not a staged photo. This was not a pretty, lithe woman in an empty cemetery. This was a real woman, dressed simply in jeans and a black top, crumpled before the headstone. Looking at this photo, I felt as if the sun were on my back, the chill blades of grass crushed beneath me, gravity holding me to the ground.

Thinking about these photos on a drive to Portland a few days later, I realized that my main emotion was...jealousy. Then, with a shock, I realized that this isn't normal. Most people do not view photos of grieving women and feel envy. While I can pass in the regular world, I really am not normal.

Why was I envious? Because they could go to their loved ones' graves. They could be there. Perhaps their loved ones weren't cremated so as these women pressed their very bodies and flesh against the carpet of grass, they lined up with the bodies of their loved ones. It's foolish, I know. Though it may be only feet of earth separating these lovers, they are no closer than Mike and me.

CHAPTER 27

A reprieve

May 31, 2013

Since returning from Hawaii, I have felt better than at any time since the accident. I slowed down enough to collect the little, scattered pieces of myself. It feels like my soul has been poured into my body, like I inhabit it again.

I am not fool enough to think, "Oh, I made it through! Everything will be better now." But I am grateful for this reprieve, this period where life isn't so painful.

In the grief memoir I'm reading, the narrator mentioned that the second year is worse. "Great", I thought, with a tinge of sarcasm, "Something to look forward to."

I'm closing in on the one year anniversary. In an odd way, I'm almost looking forward to it. I'm not sure why. Shortly after the accident, I gave myself a year to figure stuff out. A year to be crazy. A year not to think about dating. Do I think that this anniversary will bring resolution to the grief? To these questions?

Am I expecting him to return on that date? Perhaps it's a remnant of our history of deployments, always looking forward to a return date.

I won't know until I get there, until that sad anniversary arrives. Just like I don't know what the second year holds or what tomorrow holds. But I am grateful for today.

CHAPTER 28

"I am loved"

June 1, 2013

On Thursday, there was a card addressed to Mike in the mailbox. It had Hallmark embossing on the back, but the return address was the mall. Curious, I opened it to find a card with a drawing of a heart and the message, "Celebrate Love". Opening the card, it was an offer from a diamond store for a free freshwater pearl bracelet with a heart charm that said, "I am loved".

My throat closed, and I started to wheeze. My mind raced. What did it mean? Was it a gift from beyond the grave? Or was I pathetic for being reduced to grasping at junk mail for messages from my dead boyfriend? How had they gotten his name? Had he purchased something there? It's a diamond store...was he looking at diamond rings? I was disturbed. It knocked me off my equilibrium. It felt intrusive.

I called the store to ask them to remove Mike from their mailing list and to discover what he had purchased there. The nice saleslady looked in the system and found his name but no address or any purchase information. She had no idea how the card had come to us. It was a mystery. I hung up the phone and suddenly wanted that bracelet. Desperately.

Today I drove an hour to the mall to pick up the bracelet. I hold the "I am loved" charm and still don't know what it means, except that the message is true. I am loved.

The week after the accident, my friends came to stay with me in shifts. After one of them left, I found a note on my fridge. It still lives there today. It reads:

"Mike LOVES you
Your family LOVES you
Your friends LOVE you
You are a gift
You are safe
You are not alone
You are <u>LOVED</u>"

Mike LOVES you.

Your Family LOVES you.

Your Friends LOVE you.

You are a gift.
You are safe.
You are not alone.
You are LOVED.

CHAPTER 29

A child's grief

June 6, 2013
Drafted on a flight from Seattle to Oakland

Waking to the 3:00 am alarm had left me groggy as I strolled the airport terminal before my early flight. In my bemused haze, one of the large, backlit advertisements clobbered me. I drifted to a stop as I read it: "No Child Should Grieve Alone." There was a photo of children taken from behind, and the background was a handwritten application. It was an advertisement for summer camps for children in grief.

I started to tear up and grabbed my camera to take a photo. In the nearly empty terminal, there was a lone woman nearby. She saw me photographing the sign and approached me. "Do you know someone who needs that camp?" "Yeah," I managed, with a close-lipped, polite smile. I ducked my head and moved a few steps away to take another photo. Her hand came into my field of vision holding a business card. "Here," she said, handing me her card. "I work in hospice. Please let me know if there's anything I can do." Her voice was so warm and caring. All of a sudden, I was crying. Not just a simple set of tears tracking down my cheeks but as Oprah used to say, the "ugly cry". I stood there in that empty terminal beside the grief camp sign sobbing, tears running down my face, head bowed, knuckles rubbing my forehead. When I looked up again, she had left.

Grief camps. Children's grief. There is so much pain in those terms. Shortly after the accident, Mike's son, Chris, attended a children's grief day camp. He was 10 years old. They did activities like writing the hard emotions on raw eggs to throw at a tree and writing messages to their loved one to release in balloons. One of the messages Chris wrote to his dad was, "Your friends are still riding motorcycles for you." So much poignancy in that statement.

In that timeframe, I asked my grief class facilitator if she had any recommendations for children's grief resources. She sent me to the Sesame Street website. I was surprised to find that they have a whole section on children's grief. Digging into it, I found a number of printable booklets, including one for grieving children in military families. What a touching publication. One of the things it said was that even if your loved one didn't die in combat, they are still a hero. While this is a book for children, this statement has been comforting for me as well.

One day the grief class facilitator asked me to meet her before the class. She had brought stacks of books for children in grief. I quickly flipped through them, sampling the tone and message, until I found one I liked: *The Boy Who Didn't Want to Be Sad.* It's not specifically about grief but about dealing with uncomfortable emotions. The boy comes up with a plan to remove everything in his life that makes him sad. Eventually, he realizes that he also removed everything that makes him happy. One of the reviews says, "This is a book about facing sadness so that we can also have a happy and fulfilled life." This is what

I want for Chris. I checked with his mom then sent him a copy.

Chris is coming to visit me in a few weeks, along with his grandma and mom. When he was in Washington for the memorial service, he said that he wanted to come back and visit the next summer. I was cautiously enthusiastic. Didn't want to get my hopes up because I wasn't sure if he'd change his mind. But over the following months, his mom said that he was still talking about it, asking what the weather would be like in Washington in the summer and what he should pack. For Christmas, I sent him a card with a hand drawn gift certificate for a flight to Seattle. Still, I was unsure if it would actually happen. But about a month ago, they booked their flights. What a gift.

Now, I am in planning mode. When I asked his grandma, Mike's mom, what she wanted to do during the trip, she just said, "Show us what makes Washington a special place." No pressure! I'm making lists of possible fun activities, but in the private corner of my heart, I'm looking forward to the more bittersweet, meaningful parts of the visit. I want to show them my memory basket and the memorial bench. I want to bring them to the bike night and have the motorcycle riders make them feel special. I want to connect with Chris in a way that's not possible over the phone.

I wish I could take the pain away and make it all better. The truth is that I can't even say, "I understand." I've never been a young man who lost his dad too early. All I can do is accompany Chris on his grief journey, share my stories and listen to his, and try to be a good companion.

Early morning, Seatac airport

CHAPTER 30

Sleeping loud

June 9, 2013

Traveling can be hard. I'm in California now for work and a family visit. Compulsively, I check my phone for texts and emails from Mike. I want to call him. It feels like he's waiting at home for me to return.

Friday night, I dreamt of him, for only the third or fourth time. He was a dark figure sitting behind a desk in a shadowy home office. I shuffled in, small and frail and embarrassed and needy. "I've been good; I haven't asked for anything for a really long time... Could I please just have a hug?" God, I wanted that hug, his warm arms and solid chest enveloping me. I woke before he could respond and lay in the dark...yearning. I rolled over and tried to go back to sleep, only to find little mewling noises coming from my throat.

I call this "sleeping loud". From about three to six months after the accident, I slept loud. All the emotions that daylight wouldn't allow emerged in the darkness of my bedroom. In the space between sleep and wakefulness, I heard growls, wheezing, moans, and little mewling whines of pain. Grieving is so much work. Day and night, processing, integrating, rolling through emotions, swimming through memories, crawling and grasping for survival. It is not for the timid.

The book from my grief class discussed "keening". I imagine it as an uncontrolled animal sound, ripped from your soul and translated through your body. Not emanating from the body but passing through it only as a vessel. A couple of the people in my class described their experiences keening. I was jealous for such a release. Our group facilitator suggested that I might have that experience in the future, that I should go into the woods and try it. I haven't. It seems too staged and self-conscious.

But simply knowing that keening is a possibility, I give myself permission to sleep loud. Those noises I make in the still of the night, those are the raw, unfiltered core of grief. Those are the uncensored truth of the experience that words cannot encompass.

CHAPTER 31

Motorcycle school prelude

June 18, 2103
Drafted on a flight from Seattle to Salt Lake City

I am flying to Salt Lake City now, heading towards the Yamaha Champions Motorcycle School. This trip is a long time coming. I signed up for it in February, the day after the dedication for Mike's memorial park bench. The class seemed so distant that it would never come, which was fine with me.

I've made it through the time since the accident by moving from one event in his honor to the next. There was the memorial service in September, then the track day (that we were supposed to do together), then the Halloween 5k (that I ran in his honor in the costume from our first Halloween together), then the memorial bench, then the burial, and finally, this school. I feel like an ice climber, planting an ice ax, then hanging on for dear life on that slick, perilous surface until the next ax is planted. Just keep focused on the next step, then the next, then the next, and someday I'll look up and be okay.

In many ways, this trip makes NO sense. Here I am, a

woman traveling alone across state lines for an intensive motorcycle class. Who does this? No one I know - and especially not
novice riders. But in another way, it's the only thing that makes
sense.

I live in two worlds simultaneously. In the real world, the
fact that I ride at all is nonsensical. In the parallel world, "down
the rabbit hole", life post-accident is strange and scary and bi-
zarre. In this world, the *only* things that make sense are the things
that I'm doing for Mike, in his honor. While my logical brain
questions my decision-making, my heart knows that each of
these steps is necessary.

I've done everything I can to prepare for the class. Over the
months, I've moved from dire nerves to a sense of calm purpose
(still mixed with nerves, truth be told). Now is the time to
breathe deeply and be present. To show up with a sense of hu-
mility and a hunger to learn. I know that Mike would be proud
of me for moving through my fear and doing this class. And I
know at the end of the experience, I will be extremely grateful.

I signed up for this class because it was something that I had
always wanted to do with Mike. Now I'm taking it for Mike. He
would be thrilled for me. I want to soak up the experience for
both of us. I want to carry him forward with me, not living my
life for him, but sharing my experiences with him. Living a life
that he would respect. I still want to make him proud.

Postscript...

It had occurred to me before this trip that normally, when
women travel with a garment bag, they're holding a wedding
dress, not motorcycle leathers. Today, no fewer than three people at the airport mistook my leathers for a wedding dress. They
were excited for me and concerned about it getting wrinkled. I

just laughed when the flight attendant kicked the bag to get it into the closet on the airplane. The leathers are made to take much more abuse than that! And no worries about wrinkles. In some ways, leathers are much more practical than a wedding dress. Not that I wouldn't trade them in a heartbeat if I could.

A couple friends of ours, also motorcycle riders, got married over the weekend. The wedding photos brought tears to my eyes. He held her with such care on the dance floor, and the love poured out of his eyes, making his face look all misty and blurry, like a young boy entranced with an angel.

Once upon a time, Mike looked at me that way. I will never settle for less than that again. If I am to love in the future, it will be a real love. I refuse to settle for less than magic, now that I've experienced it.

CHAPTER 32

Motorcycle school completed

June 21, 2013
Drafted on a flight from Salt Lake City to Seattle

Well...I survived! On a different bike, first time on this track, with new instructors and challenging drills, I made it. First things first - a sigh of relief and, just possibly, a little self-congratulation. It was really hard, sometimes frustrating, a few moments when I wanted to give up, but it was totally, completely, and utterly worth it. Without a doubt.

The morning of the first day, we introduced ourselves. Our class of 20 had five women, including me. Four of the five of us came alone, and the one woman in a couple was the person who got her boyfriend into riding, not vice versa. Since I had felt like such a freak when I booked the school, it was interesting to see that I wasn't so weird after all.

Our class was an interesting group, ranging from early 20's to mid-60's, Several doctors, a patent lawyer, an archaeologist, a special ed teacher. We ranged in skill and experience from me and a couple others with only a couple years riding to several active racers.

When I introduced myself, I was feeling emotional so I explained about Mike. "I'd like to share something personal. One of the reasons I'm here is that I always wanted to take this school with my boyfriend, but he died last August in a motorcycle accident the day after he returned from deployment. But I figured that I could still come. So if you see me getting emotional, that's what it's about, and it'll pass." Once I got it out, I felt better, and I didn't end up crying at all during the class. (Though I must admit that a couple times I was so frustrated that I wanted to cry! But that's different.)

The school was very fast paced, both in the classroom and on the track. I don't mean that we had to speed on the track, but we moved quickly from one exercise to the next. I didn't have much time to think about Mike, which was probably a good thing. I really needed to focus on what I was doing.

Yet again, like on the street, I was the slowest one out there. Sigh. But the instructors were wonderful. I couldn't keep up with the first group they assigned me. No problem; they just split two of us off, and we got our own instructor. Score! Plenty of one-on-one attention.

Every single skill we worked on was something completely new to me so it was all challenging at first. But I stuck with it and found myself with burgeoning skills in areas where I had zero ability earlier, most noticeably in trail braking and body position. There were moments going around the corners where I thought to myself in amazement, "Hey, I'm doing this! Boy, I wish Mike could see me. He would be so proud. He would be thrilled."

Of course, there were also moments of, "Damn, I suck. I hate this. If I hadn't paid so much for such a short period of time (two days), I'd just go in and take a break." But I stuck with it and did my best on all the drills and exercises. And the persistence paid off.

The instructors were unfailingly supportive and encouraging, pointing out all of my successes. I sopped up the praise and thumbs up. I'm actually kind of embarrassed at how much it meant to me. I just miss getting that support and encouragement from Mike.

On both days, the instructors videoed each one of us, then the class reviewed the film, with the instructors giving a running commentary on what each rider did well and which habits could be dangerous. There were a total of six instructors, with a mind-blowing collection of racing resumes. The film review sessions ended up feeling like a group of friends kibitzing in one of their garages. Fun, supportive, and with a TON of experience reviewing YOU. I learned so much in those sessions, from watching the other riders as well as myself.

While watching the film, I found myself wishing we were reviewing Mike's film. He would have loved the school, just eaten it up. It would have been such an amazing experience to share with him.

Now, flying home, I so wish that I could discuss the school with him. I wish I could tell him all about it and see his eyes light up. I wish I could hear his thoughts. We knew each other so well that most of the time, I could anticipate what he was going to say, but sometimes he would surprise me. It makes me sad that I'll never be surprised by his insights again.

Overall, I am so grateful for this experience. I am leaving here with skills that I never would have developed any other way. With improved confidence. While I couldn't see the logic in attending this school before I came, I do now. It was a completely appropriate tribute to Mike. It gives me insight into him and what he loved so much about riding. While on the track, I felt just a glimmer of how the motorcycle used to feel when we rode two-up. This is the first time I have ever been able to give myself that sensation on the bike. I actually didn't think it was possible. Three years I've been riding, and this is the first time that the bike has ever felt even the slightest bit like it did with him. I'll take it, even just that little taste, with gratitude and love.

Postscript: (drafted later in the day)

It was so hard walking in the house after returning from the airport. I wanted to open the door and see Mike waiting here for me. The "never again" part of his loss is still hard to understand. It's not just that I can't talk to him now, it's never again. It's never another hug. Ugh. It makes me feel all panicky. I can't think that far ahead. Back in December, my mantra was, "He's not here today, and he won't be here tomorrow." That was as far ahead as I could look. Now I can look a couple months ahead. But "never again"? I'm not okay with that. Really, really not.

Riding at the Yamaha Champions Riding School. Photo credit: 4theriders.com

Yamaha Champions Riding School, Miller Motorsports Park, Utah

CHAPTER 33

My body

July 1, 2013

Here's a post that I'm embarrassed to write. Honestly, I have no idea why. I've already shared with you the noises I make in the middle of the night and my inappropriate thoughts in social situations. What's left to be embarrassed about? So...here goes nothing...

I am thinking about getting nude portraits taken. There, I said it.

I've had such a strange relationship with my body since the accident. At first, I wanted to be invisible, and I dressed that way. A uniform of jeans and unstyled hair, for all occasions except the memorial service, where I wanted Mike to be proud of me.

A few months later, I experimented with being seen. I dressed up (though still didn't do my hair). In an odd way, I was angry at my body - or perhaps *through* my body. I would throw the clothes on, not with care, but with recklessness. "Take this," I would say to myself, dressing quickly in jeans that were a little too tight or a skirt that was a little too short. They were always with a nice top. The type of outfits where you'd wonder if the woman knows that her jeans are too tight because the entire effect is classy but slightly off.

In that period, I had daydreams of going to the bar a couple of miles away and picking up a man. With anger, or aggression, or passion (perhaps with desperation), I would force him to see me. I would throw my body at him like a dirty rag, like something useless, valueless. I'd tell him, "There's nothing wrong with my body! See? This body still deserves love." Of course, I did no such thing.

Mike loved my body. He gazed at me with bone deep appreciation. His eyes would light up when he saw me naked. For some reason, this man, the most observant person I've ever met, completely missed all my flaws. There is something so reassuring about being naked, defenseless, vulnerable before someone you love and having them appreciate all of you. And truly SEE all of you.

My life now is filled with surface social interactions. I miss being truly seen and appreciated, physically and emotionally. I feel invisible much of the time. In the same vein as the "tree falling in the forest" saying, I wonder if I can be desirable in the absence of someone desiring me.

These portraits will not be for others. The purpose is not to entice. The purpose is to record, to reflect back. I wonder what I will see in these photos. Will I see a broken woman? A woman with value? With something left to offer? With strength, beauty, heart?

When I imagine the photos, I think of the gorgeous black and white nudes of breast cancer survivors with mastectomies. Their scars are visible. Will mine be?

Lately, I've been coming to terms with the fact that I'm still alive, that I still exist. Will I even show up in the photos? Perhaps seeing myself from an outside perspective will help me understand that I still inhabit this earth, this body.

I haven't taken any steps to arrange the portraits. A few years ago, I offered Mike to have some professional nudes taken of me with his bike as a welcome back gift when he returned from deployment. He thanked me but turned me down. He didn't want anyone else seeing me naked. Having the photos taken now...it will be a conscious decision to go against his wishes. It may feel disloyal.

Loyalty is part of this body image debate. Whose body is it? Of course, it's always been mine, but it was reserved, gladly, for him alone. If I choose to share it with someone else, even just visually, is that a transgression?

Logically, I know that he is gone. This whole argument is fallacious, moot. But the heart doesn't always follow the head. I am not free to follow my own path until my heart releases me. Eventually, I will probably do the portraits, either as self-portraits or professionally. I hope that these portraits show who I am becoming. That through the body, I may gain insight into the soul.

CHAPTER 34

A violent revolt

July 2, 2013

Since returning from the motorcycle school, my body has been in a violent revolt against me. I returned on a Friday. Sunday morning, I woke with a slightly swollen lip. "Bummer," I thought. "I must have been bitten by a spider in my sleep." I joked about it with my friends at the track. (That was my track day, scheduled to practice my newfound skills on my own bikes.)

By Monday, the swelling had continued. It was mildly funny. It now looked like I had had lip injections. I texted a photo to a friend with the quip, "If I were to choose one procedure to have, it wouldn't be lip augmentation!" (I come pre-set with big lips.) But all jokes aside, the swelling was also worrisome.

I went in to see the doc. She diagnosed it as stress induced (combined with the hot, dry Utah weather at the school) and gave me a prescription. The next few days weren't funny at all. My lips were so swollen that I looked in the mirror and saw a freak. I saw one of those visions used to scare kids in health class.

I was crushed. "At least Mike's not here to see me like this," crossed my mind regularly, alternating with a fervent wish for him to come take care of me. I felt unlovable. Both then and in the future.

My body continued to spiral downward. As my lips slowly healed, a rash popped up on my arm and a few days later, it started on my eyelids. In the middle of a heat wave, it was close to 90 in my house as I prepared for bed. I called a friend in tears, overwhelmed with the heat and the swelling, stinging, and itching. "Should I go to urgent care?" We talked for a bit, and I decided to wait for morning.

Back to the doc I went. She took one look at me, "What have you been doing to yourself?!" "I don't know," I said, putting on a brave face. But the tears were only partially buried under the surface. She sent me off with more potent prescriptions and an emergency appointment with the ophthalmologist. Turns out that it's dangerous to have infections near your eyes. He gave me a clean bill of health, with a warning to come in "tout de suite" at the first sign of redness.

What a mess.

It turns out that there's a limit to the amount of stress I can take, and I have to respect that. My anxiety was off the charts, both leading up to the school and while attending. I did everything I could to bring it down but just couldn't get it to a manageable level. Then I returned to an intense work schedule, nerves about the track day, a huge emotional load with Mike's family set to arrive Friday, and concern about the looming memorial ride to the accident site in two weeks.

I thought I was okay, but my body knew better. It's on a bad path. I have to catch my breath and get my equilibrium back. I

have to end this revolt, not by bulling through the pain and anxiety but by soothing and comforting and babying myself. This
goes against the grain. I am not friends with my body now. But
we can't survive as opponents. We need to come to some resolution, some peace. And soon. Mike's son and mom arrive in
two days.

CHAPTER 35

A grief collage

July 2, 2013

After coming back from Hawaii, my mom started the grief class. Hallelujah. I'm so grateful and so proud of her. When I enrolled, I was still in shock, in crisis. It was only four weeks after the accident. I didn't have time to build up any fear or resistance to going. Mom, on the other hand, has had 10 months to process since the accident. For her to attend means that she is consciously stepping into that uncomfortable, fearful, painful space. That is courageous.

Since she started the class, I've had weekly check-in conversations with her during our regular lunch dates. Each week, she looks totally wrung out. It's hard but worthwhile. And she keeps going back. It's so wonderful to be able to talk about the class with her. We've talked more about death, grief, and Mike in the weeks since she started the class than we had in the months prior.

The class has weekly homework assignments. Last week, her assignment was to make a collage about the grief experience. Mom hasn't done it yet. I encouraged her to do it and explained

how valuable I found it, even though I didn't throw mine together until the hour before the class. In a spurt of openness, I
offered to share mine.

My collage hangs in Mike's closet, above the plastic bin with
the few things I kept of his. I can't bear to use the closet for
anything else. Though it makes no sense, I keep my clothes in
the guest room closet. The closet in the bedroom houses his
memories.

Pulling the collage off the wall, my chest tightened. I placed
it on the coffee table in front of my mom, and she silently surveyed it, nodding her head. "How does it make you feel?" She
asked. "It's perfect," I said. "It perfectly captures where I was
at that point." My eyes welled up. "Thank you for sharing it with
me," she said. In the past, she would have rejected the ugly emotions on the page, but I see a difference in her now. I am grateful. It makes it possible for me to share more of the totality of
this experience with her.

And here is the collage, assembled roughly six weeks after
Mike's death:

Grief collage

Not surprisingly, some of what I wanted to express wasn't available in pre-printed text from magazines. Undeterred, I wrote out the words in permanent ink on lined paper.

The collage is titled "Last Page", and the center is dominated by a huge question mark with the slogan "what to do" astride it. Pinwheeling from it are the emotions blankness, panic, terror, and alienation. Across the word "alienation", it says, "outsider".

I felt such power and fear pasting these words on the page. These words are not socially acceptable. As soon as these joined the page, I knew that I could not show this collage publicly. But they were also the rock-bottom absolute truth of my experience at that point.

In the upper left corner, it says "goodbye", and below that is a card someone sent me. It depicts a figure bowed with grief, before a yellow rose laid across a rock. His figure is almost indistinguishable from the polished river rocks.

When I received the card, at first I didn't see the figure, then suddenly I did, and my breath stopped. A huge upwelling of emotion followed. "I know that feeling," I thought. It was like a physical representation of my shattered heart. His surrender to grief was something that I could not do, as I walked upright through my days in bewilderment. With everyone complimenting me on my strength. "You do not see my weakness, my pain, my crushed spirit," I would say silently to them with beseeching eyes. "My strength is a sham. This figure, bent wholly in two, rocking back and forth with his crossed legs...this is the truth."

    To the upper right is a lit match, burning the word "home". Beneath that, I pasted "loneliness". In the grief class, someone asked what this meant. "My home life went up in flames," I told her. There is no subtext here.

In the center bottom of the page is a series of phrases cut
from motorcycle magazines. I just grabbed anything that hit me
in the gut. Here's what it says:

"The myth of safety
It's not a movie
NOBODY protects riders
BMW S1000RR"

This is about coming to terms with the accident, with the
stripping away of the veil of safety, the "it won't happen to us"
prayer and myth that every rider embraces. I had always wondered about riders' perceptions of risk and safety. Now I felt
like a living experiment on the subject. And the BMW is the bike
he was riding.

And finally, in the bottom right corner, is the small glimmer of hope. Even using the word glimmer is too strong. It was like the faintest wash of watercolor you could imagine, barely perceptible. Yet, I could not, in good conscience, complete the collage without acknowledging gratitude and hope. This section says:

"Me and my bike
Have the audacity to believe
Gratitude"

I still don't entirely understand this section, though it rings just as true in my heart today as it did when I pasted the words on the page. The first two lines are about my riding, though months later, I still cannot articulate why I ride. Why I did not repudiate motorcycles in the aftermath of the trauma.

And it is fitting that the final word on the poster is "gratitude". As strange as it might sound to an outsider, this experience showed me how much love surrounds me in a way that I never knew before. I was awed by the outpouring and generosity of close friends, acquaintances, and pure strangers. During this period, I felt gratitude so deeply, it was almost painful. It overwhelmed me, like a huge wave capturing me in the undertow, with each tiny grain of kindness.

Yes, while there are no words to describe how horror-filled this experience has been, I stand by my decision to close the poster with "gratitude". It does not lessen the weight of the heavy parts of the experience. But it is no less true because there is pain. Gratitude is my endcap, my bookend. Like the collage, I choose to end this post with Gratitude.

CHAPTER 36

What's your poison?

July 9, 2013

A few months ago, someone on the motorcycle forum posted a thread titled, "What's your poison?" He asked what you found yourself unable to resist doing. Most people gave responses like eating ice cream, playing video games, drinking coffee, and riding motorcycles. Me? My poison is the damn motorcycle forum. And Facebook. And my email accounts. And texts.

It's an endless round of checking for new messages. I'm not consciously looking for messages from Mike, but underneath it all...yes. It's a strange compulsion. I press the "new posts" button over and over again. Switch from one website to the next, looking for messages. When I get one from someone, anyone, it appeases the hunger for a few moments, until I start searching again. It is sad. It is pathetic. It is an addiction.

For months I have told myself, "It doesn't matter how many times you check, there will never be another message from him." But it doesn't stick. Even when I get "messages", like the "I am loved" bracelet, I still keep searching the websites. So much of our relationship was electronic. When he wasn't here in person, I waited for his messages.

I have held off on writing any messages to him. But really, the motorcycle school review I wrote was a message to him. The reason it was so long is that it contained all the stories I wanted to share with him. I wanted so badly to tell him about it when I returned.

This week, his mom and son are here. We talk quite openly about Mike. Whenever his son finds something fun or funny, he says, "I bet my dad is laughing right now." Today on the drive home from Hurricane Ridge and Lake Crescent, Chris was getting silly from too many hours in the car, singing "I'm too silly for my shirt." We laughed and joked about how silly his dad was. "He was 100% silly," Chris said.

For some reason, this triggered an intense longing. "No, not 100% silly," I thought to myself and remembered a non-silly moment. A moment when Mike was serious, when he looked at me with caring and love and reached out to touch me. He made me feel so loved and safe.

Later in the evening while fetching our carry-out dinner, I realized that I still haven't 100% decided if I want to continue in this life. It's going on a year, and it still hurts this badly? Aarrggh. I'm not going to do anything about it. But I'm still not 100% committed to life.

Tonight I find myself searching harder than ever. Hitting those refresh buttons over and over. And there are no messages to assuage the pain and anxiety. So instead, I'm writing it out, writing out the pain and anxiety. Perhaps there is some consanguinity between the poison of my searching on the Internet and the healing of my posting on the Internet.

CHAPTER 37

Ride report one: memorial ride

This section is a little different. Rather than a blog post, this is a ride report, originally shared on the pnwriders.com motorcycle forum. It is edited here for brevity...and also to add more of the personal side.

You'll find that the tone of the ride reports is a bit different than the blog posts. This is because the blog posts were anonymous, and the ride reports were posted under my name. Still, while the writing is different, I wanted to include the ride reports because they are an important part of my journey. The blog posts reflect the internal journey, and the ride reports offer a glimpse into the external journey.

In the motorcycle community, memorial rides are held to honor fallen riders. They are a way to pay tribute through doing something that the rider loved.

This memorial ride was a three-day trip to visit the memorial marker that Mike's friends and I had placed at the accident site. There were six of us on the ride, including the three friends who were with him at the accident.

July 18, 2013

Before setting off, I had no idea how I would do. I imagined Mike giving one of his loose shrugs and saying, "Well, we'll see how THIS goes!"

This trip was a lot of firsts for me. First overnight trip, first ride over 150 miles, first time over 75 mph, first time south of Port Orchard (I live 15 minutes north), first time on I5, first time on the BMW longer than 75 miles, first time riding in a city I didn't know, first time on the BMW in the dark... Well, you get the idea.

I privately named this trip the "face your demons" ride. Of course, there were the personal demons of the accident site, staying at the hotel where we met the guys the night before the accident, and gassing up at the station where I last saw him alive. Then there were the riding challenges. But I generally accomplish what I put my mind to so I was willing to go for it. I really wanted to do this trip. And it was an absolutely amazing experience.

Day One:

Bremerton, WA to Baker City, OR

I haven't had many dreams of Mike since the accident, but I have one just before waking. It isn't anything personal - he was in a great mood and was laughing about some bike's geometry – but it puts me in a hopeful, upbeat mood setting off this morning.

I haven't looked at the route closely, other than seeing the total mileage and shuddering, so it is a surprise when we head to the Tacoma Narrows Bridge. Feeling like a doofus for not being better prepared, I fumble out my ghetto wallet (ziplock bag) and hand the whole thing to the toll lady. "Please take what you need," I ask her with a sheepish smile. "I'm sorry I'm not better prepared." She smiles and carefully counts out the six dollars. This is my first time crossing the bridge on my bike.

At this point, it dawns on me that we must be going to I5, my nemesis. Well, at least it's early on a Sunday morning so traffic shouldn't be too heavy. We'll see how this goes! We only stay on I5 for about 15 minutes. Not my favorite place but no scary incidents either. Not bad for my first time on I5.

Soon enough, we get to our first interesting road of the day, Highway 25. It's beautiful up here, but this road is a tease. It's fun, but I can't relax because of the poor pavement quality. I decide that I love the suspension on the BMW – no bottoming out like Mike and I did riding this road together on the Sprint ST.

Highway 25, Washington. Photo credit: Brad Everett

Heading south, south, south, eventually we run along the Columbia River. Pretty! Fun little tunnels! I like the way the bikes sound in the tunnels – kind of like a reverse Doppler Effect since I am in the back.

Pretty soon we're at the Hood River Bridge. Ugh – long

metal grate bridge. Brad helpfully mentions on the headset that you can see the water through the bridge deck. No thank you! I carefully do NOT look down.

After crossing the bridge, we roll along towards Condon, Oregon, and the temperature rises. The dry fields and windmills are beautiful. As we wind our way along, the road is in great condition, but I'm a little intimidated by the red chunky gravel on the shoulder before the drop-off so I keep things nice and mellow.

I glance in my mirror, and Mark's not there. Hmmm... I slow down, then really slow down. A couple turns later, he's still not there. I pull over in the gravel (yuck, hate gravel) and have a moment of panic imagining him having slid through the gravel and over the embankment. (Not likely at my wussy speed, but you never know.)

I sit there a few moments and consider my options. Take out my phone and try to call the riders ahead? Go back and look for him? A minute later, he rolls up. Thank God. I take off, accidentally doing a nice burnout in the gravel. We pull up to the other riders at the mountain marker, and I take a moment to gather myself and shake it off.

By the time we get to Condon, I'm hot and hungry and wiped out. We stop for gas, where the guys help me figure out the old pumps, and I ask Brad to take a photo. This is a meaningful photo.

Condon, Oregon. Photo credit: Brad Everett

Three years ago, when Mike's bike broke down in Condon on their road trip, I drove all night to deliver another bike. The next morning, I watched them through the window of the market as they left town and was caught in a vivid daydream. In it, I was riding with the group on a white bike as we pulled out of the Condon gas station.

I kept this vision quietly in my heart. It seemed so farfetched that I would ever get to the point that I could join a group of good riders on a long trip. At that point, I was only a few months past my basic motorcycle safety course and was still doing parking lot practice. But I kept that dream alive, thinking through the years as I practiced and practiced that I would tell Mike about it if it ever came true. Little did I know it would be on his memorial ride. This is heavy in my heart as we stop at the deli and order sandwiches and milkshakes.

Lunch in Condon, Oregon

I'm not looking forward to our destination of Baker City. Several hours – and several hundred miles – later, we roll through town past the Geiser Grand Hotel, where Mike and I spent our last night together, and pull in at the Best Western.

Best Western, Baker City, Oregon

What are the odds that the dates we picked for the trip would overlap with the Hells Canyon motorcycle rally? Feeling emotional, I decide that it's fitting – a motorcycle rally coinciding with a memorial ride. There's a poster board for the rally set out in the lobby with pens beside it, and I kneel and write in tiny script, "RIP mikefsu". I don't think they'll mind a small note of respect to a fallen rider.

We eat dinner at the hotel restaurant, just one table over from where we all ate dinner the night before the accident. So strange to think that it's almost been a year.

Day Two:
Baker City, OR to Eugene, OR

The next morning, it's surreal to see my bike sitting outside the hotel. I rode that thing 500 miles yesterday? Get outta here! And I'm not nearly as sore as I expected.

Leaving the Best Western, we gas up at the station beside it, which is where I last saw Mike. As we leave town, I'm glad to have faced these demons. They've lost some of their power over me, and I feel more at peace.

Our first destination of the day is the memorial site. As I park and walk towards it, I want to be anywhere but here. But there have also been many times when I've wished I could come here. It is good to be back, to see that the marker is still in good condition.

I have some chores to take care of so I set to them. I had offered his family to bring anything down that they wanted to leave at the marker. His son brought me a Chewbacca Lego with a chainsaw. Mike used to make Chewbacca noises, and Chris just liked the chainsaw. I place them on the crossbeam. His mom gave me some recent laminated photos of Chris, and I attach them to the upright. I leave a couple cards at the base. Next, I take some pencil rubbings of the plaque for myself and his family. We add some fresh flags to the marker, and it is all set.

Memorial marker, Highway 26 outside Unity, Oregon

Chewbacca with a chainsaw

The accident site looks just as I remember it – spare, harsh, and beautiful. The only sounds are the wind, an antelope, and a hawk. There are still pieces of the bike scattered about, and Blake finds an intact headlight bulb. With the ferocity of the accident, it's strange to find such a fragile piece intact. I file it under the heading of yet another thing that doesn't make sense about the accident and tuck it in my tank bag. We say a few words at the marker then trudge back to the bikes to continue on. As we pull away, my spirit lightens. It's always good to face your demons.

The rest of the day is a blur. The variety of fantastic roads in this part of the country is eye opening. We pass through fields, canyons with big sweeping turns, forests, mountain passes, and everything in between. The highest ambient temp my bike shows is 97, and I learn that it's always good to keep extra water on you when I run out.

I'm looking at the view from Highway 52, Oregon. Photo credit: Brad Everett

I'm more and more grateful for the skills I learned at the Yamaha Champions Riding School a couple weeks ago. With this many miles and variety of terrain, the trip is fantastic practice. I learn to relax and have fun in the open, sweeping corners. Following Blake over Highway 52 is a total blast. The bike feels more like it did riding with Mike than it ever has before.

Then we hit Highway 242, and I learn that I still have a long way to go when it comes to dealing with the tight twisties. I find this road intimidating with the narrow lanes and oncoming traffic. Let's just say that this is not my finest moment. I decide that I just need to survive this road so I ride extra slowly. Someday I'll return to McKenzie Pass and show it what's up – when I have a few more miles under my belt.

My slow progress over Highway 242, Oregon. Photo credit: Brad Everett

As the day winds to a close, we roll towards Eugene. I mentally cross my fingers that finding the hotel will be easy. I'm nervous about riding in a new town. Well, it's not a big town, but it has a confusing layout so we spend about an hour crisscrossing it looking for the hotel. It ends up being good for me because eventually I shake off the nerves and realize that it is just riding, and I am okay. Darkness falls, and I also get some good nighttime riding experience.

We arrive at the motel a little after 10:00 pm. Immediately, all the guys pull out their phones to call their wives and girlfriends. My kneejerk reaction is to pull out my phone and check in with Mike. I remind myself, "That's not for you now." Then I realize that it will never be for me. I will never call him to check in again. I sit on the curb outside the motel room and let my shoulders slump.

Day Three:

Eugene, OR to Bremerton, WA

This day brings more interesting roads, though it's much cooler, with wet pavement and some sprinkles in the morning. The road by Alsea Falls is beautiful, and Highway 53...what an amazing road. I understand why Washington riders would come down to Oregon just to ride that highway.

Alsea Falls, Oregon. Photo credit: Brad Everett

I only have one scary passing experience of the trip – not bad considering that I had only passed a couple times before this trip. In a legal passing zone on a two-lane country road, the white SUV doesn't want me to pass. He speeds up as I'm passing him. There is a cross street ahead, and a red truck approaches on the cross street and starts to turn right into the lane I am occupying. "Oh shit!" I duck back behind the SUV and take some deep breaths. A little spooked, I am more conservative with my passing the rest of the day.

We stop in Tillamook for a late lunch at 3:30 then in Astoria for gas. The Astoria Bridge is a crazy high bridge! I am nervous approaching it, but as we cross it, I can't help but be blown away by the beauty of the water, boats, and birds riding the wind. It is like being in a low flying airplane. As we approach our "landing" of the bridge running low across the water, a sense of peace falls over me. This trip is a completely appropriate tribute to Mike.

Astoria Bridge, Oregon. Photo credit: Brad Everett

In the late afternoon sun, the sweeping turns along the water are gorgeous. The ride home is fast and fun. (Well, fast for me. I'm sure it isn't for the guys.) Though my hands and knees are sore, I feel relaxed and comfortable.

Arriving home, I take extra care pulling into my gravel alleyway. "I'll be damned if I'm going to drop this thing in my own alley after riding 1,400 miles," I tell myself. After getting the bike turned around in my driveway, I shut it off and throw up my arms triumphantly. "I did it!" Looking at the gorgeous moon and the last light of the setting sun, I feel such gratitude.

This trip was another step in coming to terms with Mike's death – and an important one. I never could have done it without the support of these wonderful friends. They took my bike to the dealership the week before when the fuel pump went out, installed my aftermarket goodies at the last minute when it came back, lubed my chain at the hotels, pumped my gas when I was hot and tired and couldn't figure out the old Oregon pumps. They led me and followed me for all of the 1,400 miles. They waited for me in the heat – then waited longer so that I could take a needed break too after catching up. They supported me and encouraged me and made me feel like a welcome part of the group. The motorcycle community is amazing.

CHAPTER 38

Memorial ride aftermath

July 20, 2013

Sunday through Tuesday I rode 1,400 miles in three days with Mike's friends to visit the memorial site. It is shocking how well it went, given how little experience I had with long rides. My longest day prior was 150 miles. We did 500 miles on the first day of the trip. This post is about the aftermath.

When we first returned, I was riding high on the afterglow. Wednesday and Thursday I felt loose and happy. I wrote a ride report of the trip and read it over and over again. The trip went by so fast, it seemed unreal.

Yesterday, reality hit with a bang, triggered by washing my car, of all things. It was a gorgeous summer day so I left work early to wash my bike, filthy from the trip. As long as I was washing, I decided to do my car. This is only the second time I have washed it myself since the accident. It's actually only my second time EVER washing it. Mike always took care of it.

Washing it is an admission that he isn't coming back. No matter how long I wait, how dirty it becomes, he will not be back to clean it. I was so mad.

After cleaning it, I sat down and cleaned my motorcycle leathers, covered with splattered bugs. As I vigorously rubbed the leather with the cleaner and rag, a sense of pent-up futility welled up. There's not a damn thing I can do to make him come back. Even performing unheard-of feats of riding with the long days of the trip...it doesn't matter. I could become a motorcycle racer, the most skilled woman rider ever (well, actually I probably couldn't, but even if I did), it wouldn't make a damn bit of difference.

Ashes to ashes, dust to dust. He is in that quiet field in Kansas. The vitality that filled him...I don't know where it is. It bothers me that I just don't KNOW. Is he truly gone? A simple snap out of existence, like pressing "stop" at the end of a movie? Is he here on my shoulder, my guardian angel? Is he in heaven, wherever and whatever that is? Is he asleep, waiting for God to awaken him? Or has he been reborn into his next body? The not knowing eats at me.

This morning, I joined some friends crabbing on the Puget Sound. As the boat skimmed across the water, the wind pressed against me, its rough texture rubbing my face and whipping my hair about. The cold air snuck up my sleeves and tickled my forearms. The thought appeared in my mind, "I am alive." I tasted it tentatively. Unlike the past, my reaction wasn't violent revulsion but a sense of resignation. Perhaps I am slowly coming to terms with the fact that I am alive. I am not numb anymore. Perhaps there will be a future.

I am not celebrating life. But unless I actively choose to opt out, I guess I am alive. Perhaps at some point, I will stop waiting and start living actively. I'm not there yet, but at least I can say...

"I am alive."

As much as I don't want to admit it, this is progress.

CHAPTER 39

A track day

A "track day" is an opportunity to ride on a closed course (what some would call a "racetrack"). Track day riders are not there to race; instead, they practice their skills in a controlled environment, without the hazards of riding on the road.

Control riders help keep the events safe and also provide instruction. Track day instruction typically includes classroom time and track time but no formal drills, unlike an intensive school, such as the Yamaha Champions Riding School.

My first track day was a month after Mike's accident. I attended my second track day a couple days after returning from the Yamaha Champions Riding School, to practice my new skills. This post is about my third track day.

July 29, 2013

In case this blog is too negative, I wanted to share a success. Today I took my bike out to the track for my third track day. It was fantastic.

My riding skills are continuing to come together. For the first two sessions, I just focused on relaxing and familiarizing myself with the track. In the middle of the day, I was on my game.

Everything felt smooth (at least in the corners I liked), and I applied more and more of the skills learned at the school (YCRS). By the end of the day, I started to get tired and lose focus so I left the track early the last two sessions. There's no shame in that. Better to retire from the field early and in good form than to crash.

At two separate points, control riders came up to me off the track and told me that I was doing well. What a relief! My last track day, a control rider approached me, and I was secretly hoping that he was going to say I was riding well enough to move up to the next skill level. Nope, it was the opposite. He said that another rider had reported that I looked nervous out there, and he asked if I wanted a control rider to lead me around. Of course I said "yes" and was grateful for the extra instruction, but I must admit that it took the wind out of my sails a bit. So...to hear from the control riders today that I was riding well was a big win. I'm finally gaining a modicum of competence. Hell yeah.

The other important win of the day is that I had friends there beyond Mike's friends. Some were from the bike nights that I founded months ago. Some were new friends, people from the forum I had not met in person before today. Others were people we pitted next to at the last track day. It was also great to see the instructor who taught me in the first track day in September.

I love Mike's friends. They are my dear friends now too. They will probably always be my favorite people to ride with. But being able to walk around the paddock and have friends throughout...it helped me feel that I am riding for me. I'm not just filling in for Mike at events he would have attended, like some poor stand-in double. It helped me feel that I am living my life and not trying to live his.

I have not consciously been trying to live his life, but there's a fine line between doing things in his honor and living a life for him. Today was a big step in resolving the question of how I can ride for me.

CHAPTER 40

A hug

August 5, 2013

Periodically, I want a hug so badly it's painful. Last night was one of those times. The longing for a hug pulled me out of bed at 3:00 am. In the dark intimacy of the mid-night, I wandered my small house, checked the cabinets for food to fill the hole (no luck), then settled on the couch to read for distraction.

I don't want a polite social hug. Even a good friend hug with the extra squeeze at the end wouldn't do. No, I want a hug that envelopes me, that has no pre-set, polite time limit. The type of hug that I can relax into and lower my guard, reveal my weakness. The type of hug that fills me with love and appreciation, that sees my best and forgives my mistakes and weaknesses. The hug that feels like home.

For some things, there is no substitute, and this is one of them.

CHAPTER 41

The estate

August 6, 2013

This afternoon, I will meet with the estate lawyer for possibly the last time. I have such mixed feelings. On one hand, I want this to be over. These meetings are painful. It has been almost a year. It is dragging on.

On the other hand...it is a travesty that someone's life can be boiled down to a simple series of administrative, bureaucratic procedures. Mike had a full and complete financial life. The last year has been spent finding his accounts, closing them down, selling his bikes, and consolidating everything into a single estate account. The next step is for the judge to determine how to distribute the estate.

It's like a deck of cards that made a complex house, and it has collapsed room-by-room back into its composite deck. Next, it will be passed out in chunks, and it will be like it never existed at all.

I must confess, I have a knee jerk reaction of, "But what will he do when he comes back?" Yes, I know, Know, KNOW he's not coming back. But yet, I don't. Not all the time. I did so much logistical stuff for him while he was on deployment. Much of the estate work has felt like more of the same.

This year has been spent losing him, one piece at a time. Today is just another step. Part of me wants to be done walking into the painful spaces. And part of me thinks it will be the emptiest feeling in the world when his affairs are wrapped up. All that will be left of him is the grave in Kansas and the memories in the hearts of those who love him.

CHAPTER 42

A tickle

August 8, 2013

Here is some news: I have a small tickle of interest in someone. I confessed this to a friend who asked how it made me feel. A color wheel of emotions spun past my mind's eye, with the largest emotion being...relief. I am not broken. Someday I will be able to bear another's touch, will be able to touch another without that body being irrevocably wrong.

This is not an infatuation, or a crush, or a true love. It is simply a tickle. I find myself pleased with him, perhaps flirting a bit. Of course, after the minor flirtation, I ask myself what the hell I think I'm doing. I am not ready to date so I remind myself to be cautious.

I have been waiting to feel disloyal for this tickle, but so far, it hasn't happened. I had thought that I would feel torn, haunted, when this day came. Perhaps if I acted on it, my insides would twist into a knot, but right now, I'm okay.

Another side of this is the public side. Since the accident, I have been off limits to men. Once they know my situation, they do not push or flirt. I fall into a protected category, treated somewhere between 'one of the guys' and a sister. This has been a gift – knowing that I could reach out for friendship or help without it being misconstrued – and I do not relinquish this role lightly. I don't know what comes next, once I open myself to dating. I do not know how I will be treated.

Shortly after the accident, someone told me about a coworker whose boyfriend had died. Within three months, this girl had a new boyfriend. The exact word my friend used to describe this? "Nasty." I don't want to be judged as nasty. I don't want to BE nasty. What is the time limit for dating after death to avoid nastiness? What is the timeframe to avoid judgment? Six months? One year? Two? If I start dating before this mystery deadline, will my loyalty and love for Mike be questioned?

A couple of my friends have told me that they want me to be happy, that they would not judge me for being with someone new. I feel pathetically grateful for this reassurance. I'm not sure that I wouldn't judge *myself* so it seems entirely logical that others would judge me.

Even more important than my friends telling me this, Mike's *mom* has told me this. When she came to visit, we stayed up late one night talking. She said, "You're too young not to have love in your life." She said that his family would support me and love me when that day comes. I cannot tell you what a precious and pure gift this is – to know that, when I'm ready to date, his family will not see it as an insult to his memory or to them. I am humbled. What have I done to deserve such generosity? Most people in my situation do not get this level of support. I love them very much.

For months now, I have known that there's no use dating yet. I've been in a vulnerable state. Either I'd end up taken advantage of, or if I met a wonderful man, he'd be in the unenviable position of constantly being compared to the dead boyfriend. Who can live up to that? There was no hope of a healthy relationship so I closed that part of myself off. Bit by bit, it is opening now.

I feel like a flower opening towards the light. The movement is imperceptible at any particular instant, but over time, I can see the difference. I am opening myself up to the world again. I am not as invisible as I once was.

I have no idea whether this tickle of interest is returned. And it doesn't matter. I will not be following up on it. I am not ready. But even just this small tickle, it is progress.

CHAPTER 43

In anticipation

August 17, 2013

The one year anniversary of the accident is coming up on Thursday. The anticipation is giving me anxiety. I'm irritable, distracted and just plain not the best company these days.

It's strange that with all the planning I've done this year...and all of the memorial events I've scheduled...I have nothing planned for the anniversary. I've run out of steam, run out of momentum.

I'm tired of "guilting" people into showing up for memorial events. Strictly speaking, I haven't tried to guilt anyone into attending anything. But I have planned, and invited, and strategically reminded. It was important to me to have people show up to the memorial service, the bench dedication, and the bike night for his son. It was important to do the memorial ride.

But now, it's been a year (minus four days). At some point, I need to stop publicly mourning him. For how long can I keep planning events and expecting people to show up before it's just pathetic? My self-imposed deadline is one year.

So...for the anniversary, I will just sit back and see who appears in my life. I want to be surrounded with people who really want to be there, who show up of their own volition. I hope that people come and lift me up. I hope that others still miss and grieve him too. It is lonely to feel that everyone else has successfully picked themselves up and gone on with their lives. And I am still struggling with the basic, fundamental questions of who I am, of how to live.

One year ago, I was preparing for his return, just days away. Now, I am waiting for this anniversary to arrive, with something akin to dread, but also with impatience. I want this date to hurry up and come so I can say that I survived it.

CHAPTER 44

Musings (one year minus one day)

August 21, 2013

I've been waiting to feel disloyal with my thoughts about dating, and that's not how it's gone. In an interesting twist, I feel defiant.

Walking to work yesterday, my eyes idly tracked the shirtless man jogging past me. In my head, I said to Mike, "Don't you dare say a word about this. This is your fault. I would not be looking for someone else if you were here. I do not want anyone else." Of course, the reason I feel defiant is that I also feel ashamed. Otherwise, there would be no one or nothing to defy.

The other thing I noticed is that when I walk...I'm searching. Each person that I come across, I think, "Are you the one who's going to give me my hug?" I didn't even realize that I was doing it until yesterday. With the one year anniversary tomorrow, part of me is anticipating a welcome home hug, as if the one year mark is a return date, instead of a marker of how far gone he is.

Last weekend, my brother came to visit, and we went to the naval museum in town. On one of the walls, I found a series of three photos: the sub Mike used to be on, the sub he was on when he died, and a photo of a submariner's homecoming. It was like a conveyor belt carrying me along his history, except that the final photo should have been a military funeral.

I miss him.

CHAPTER 45

An open love letter

August 22, 2013

Dear Mike,

On this morning, one year since your death, I expected to feel crushed and crumpled with pain, anguish, and loss. But instead, I woke with my heart full of love for you.

I can say this without compunction: I have never once wished that I hadn't met you. I have never regretted our life together for the pain of its loss.

Today, I honor you. Today, I remember all the good that you were. Your little kid playfulness, patience with riders learning, wicked sense of competition, protectiveness of those you love, thoughtfulness in daily life and on the special days, helpfulness with those in need, amazing ability to listen, impressive intelligence, rock solid competence, sense of adventure, and more.

I miss...

- Our tickle contests
- You coming up behind me at a party and placing your hand on my back
- Your hugs (oh yes), and kisses, and more

- The way your eyes soften and light up when you see me
- You following behind me as I ride, like a sleeping dragon, with your sexy sport bike not making it out of first gear
- Riding two-up with you
- Our adventures and plans for the future
- Your hands and broad shoulders and the feel of your warm solid legs as I tuck my fingers under your inner thighs when we ride
- Curling up in bed with you, feeling encompassed by your love

You added to my life in innumerable, immeasurable ways. I learned so much from you. My life is richer for the gift of knowing you.

Though you are not here on this earth anymore, I carry you forward. You are not forgotten. You are inscribed with indelible ink on my heart.

I love you.

CHAPTER 46

One year

August 22, 2013

One year = 12 months = 52 weeks = 365 days = X hours, minutes, seconds. It's all very quantifiable. But also meaningless, when it comes to the accident. It feels like it is eternal; the fact of the accident has always existed. I can't imagine a time when it did not color my life.

And simultaneously, it feels like it just happened moments ago, so close I could reach out and touch him, through a small disturbance in space and time.

What does a year mean?

- I can breathe now.
- I still don't know who I am. With no expectations that I will be the same as before, everything is wide open. In some ways, it's like being a little kid again. Thoughts cross my mind like, "Maybe I'll be an athlete," or "Maybe I'll be the type of woman who dresses up all the time." I am experimenting. Give it a shot, see what feels right, repeat. I'll figure it out eventually.

- I have made progress in accepting the fact of the accident. I do not rail against it like six months ago.
- The overall tenor of my life has improved. The highs are higher, and the mediums are higher. But the lows are just as low as they've ever been. And the despair that coincides with them is worse. "It's been a year and I STILL feel this way? Maybe it's hopeless. Maybe I'll be in this pain forever." Then I remind myself that time heals, and with blind faith, I trudge forward.
- I still struggle with anxiety and distraction sometimes.
- I realized that I am stronger than I thought. As much as I hated it when people called me strong, I do see it now. This year I stepped up and walked into the painful spaces again and again. Because it was the right thing to do. Sometimes because it was the only thing to do.
- My riding skills have improved tremendously. It's hard for me to see the improvement myself. But last year I was only riding the same two routes over and over again on the CBR250R. This year, I pushed myself hard. I'd say that I pushed myself out of my comfort zone, except that there was no comfort zone this year. I went to the school in Utah, started to ride my BMW F800R, completed the memorial ride, became more comfortable on group rides, and did two more track days. Next week, I will set off on a solo motorcycle trip, something that would have been inconceivable last year. I have always been interested in motorcycle touring, but it would have taken a LOT longer to get here without the accident.
- My friendships have changed this year. Some friendships blossomed that had never existed aside from a passing "I

should get to know her better" thought. Others have become more distant, and that's okay too. Perhaps we'll
grow closer again in the future.

- I started the local bike nights and reached out to the motorcycle community, and they responded wholeheartedly.
- I discovered that one of my classifications for people is
how they treated me after the accident. If you showed up
when it mattered...that's all that matters.

CHAPTER 47

The day after (aka year 2, day 1)

August 23, 2013

This morning, I haven't been able to get moving. I feel paralyzed with anxiety and aversion. I spent the past year trying to claw myself forward, one step at a time. For much of it, the goal was to make it to the one-year mark. I'm not sure why that was the goal, but it was something to work towards.

This morning, the day after the anniversary, stepping out the front door to go to work will mean picking up the burdens of life again, with no end goal. Of course, there never was a true end goal. He didn't return at the one-year mark. But now, having met the one-year mark, the path just seems endless. I will be carrying these burdens forever, my own private version of Sisyphus.

I am taking September off from work. My goal for the break is to catch my breath, to take stock, and hopefully to find renewed commitment to life.

CHAPTER 48

Anti-voyeurism

August 25, 2013

Last night, I was at a party with a new couple. I've spent plenty of time this year with couples, but they've been long-term couples. This new couple was still in the affectionate, uber-connected stage. I could look at him, and I could look at her, but I simply could not look at the two of them together. My body kept twisting away.

As I sat beside her talking, he came up behind her and slid his fingers through her hair. I not only averted my gaze, my whole head swiveled away. A few moments later, I sent a darting glance to see if he was still there. It was like standing next to a raging campfire where you have to turn your back to the fire pit to avoid breathing the super-heated air. It was dangerous.

Later, five of us were standing in a group talking, including the couple. I realized that I had actually placed my back to the couple (hard to do when standing in a circle, but somehow I managed it.) Unconsciously, my body was trying to protect me.

You know that feeling when you smell a scent from your childhood, and it immediately brings you back? This was a visual version of a scent trigger. Seeing this couple triggered an intense longing to be touched. I had forgotten how much I missed Mike playing with my hair. Their connection made me long for what I had lost in the worst way.

Voyeurism is "the practice of spying on people engaged in intimate behaviors." Is there a word for the opposite of this? Hiding from people engaged in intimate behaviors? Let's call it anti-voyeurism.

CHAPTER 49

Obnoxious pink lipstick

August 28, 2013

A couple months ago, I picked up some new lipsticks at the drug store. I thought they'd be sheer...but no, they're the most obnoxious pink you've ever seen. I put them aside to return and never got to it. Last week, I pulled them out and gave them a shot.

With the advent of the new year, I am trying to shift my focus to the future, rather than the past. I got my hair colored last week. It's now a deep espresso shade. With my pale olive skin, the bright lipstick definitely stands out.

Here's the funny thing: I have absolutely no idea if it looks good or not. Is it garish and clown-like? Or is it a bright pop of color that's playful and flattering? Does it make me look older or younger? I have no frame of reference. I could look at myself in the mirror forever with no answer to these questions.

It's in the eye of the beholder. It depends on who is looking, I suppose. In the past, I felt beautiful because I was beautiful in Mike's eyes, and that's all that mattered. Now, I don't know. Now, I have to put myself out in the world and see what others think. Wearing the lipstick is a leap of faith.

Somehow, I have to figure out how to make a life again. Taking some action - any action - is a step out of the abyss. So...if you see a girl with dark hair and bright lips, be kind to her. I'm just flailing about, trying to find a way to be okay again. Trying to make a life with meaning. Maybe the obnoxious pink lipstick is a step on that path.

CHAPTER 50

Get busy living

September 2, 2013

Yesterday, I went to a big music and arts festival. It was a surprisingly meaningful day. It started with meeting a friend of a friend for coffee. She has done a significant amount of solo motorcycle travel, and I wanted to hear her tips. It was my first time meeting her.

She bustled in 10 minutes late, apologizing. Her mom had fallen the night before and needed surgery. As she explained the situation, my heart leapt out of my chest. She was bright and beautiful, and I could see her tears bubbling under the surface. In a kinship response, my tears rose too. What an unexpected heart connection.

After we made it through introductions, we got into the nitty-gritty of motorcycle tripping logistics. I asked about safety, route planning, and GPS's. She had wonderful tips and offered tons of encouragement. Our meeting closed with her saying, "The motorcycle goddesses are smiling down on you. You are on a healing journey." "I hope so," I responded fervently.

From there, I joined my friends at the festival. We wandered through the crowds and ended up at a beer garden with a good view of a music stage and the throngs of people. I missed Mike so badly, just wanted him to come up behind me and put his arms around me. I looked down at the huge crowd and reminded myself, "No matter how hard you look, you will not find him here. As wide as the world is, with billions of people, none of them will be him. You will not find him."

Our evening closed with a comedy performance. As we sat in the dark, intimate theater, the comic shared his thoughts on relationships. His ribald comments had me laughing to the point of tears. Then he mentioned that he is getting married soon. He is 49, and this is his third marriage. As he explained it, he graciously accepts friends' "congratulations" when he is with his fiancé, but in private, he is more reserved. "We've already seen that this can go one of two ways," he said. The comic took a deep breath then looked up and uttered, "Maybe I'll get it right this time." That simple phrase took me right over the edge from tears of laughter to tears of pain.

That will be me when I start dating. "Maybe I'll get it right this time." Maybe I'll choose someone who won't die young. Maybe I'll be happy.

It's a hard road. I suppose it's one that I don't have to travel. I don't ever have to date again. I don't have to put myself out in the world again. But I refuse to live that life.

As I folded laundry last night, the thought sprang up, "get busy living, or get busy dying." Maybe that is my theme for year two. It's a little darker than I'd like, but it's true. I refuse to live a second-rate life. It is a real life or nothing. It is a life that better be worth all this bullshit.

I have been pushing, pushing, pushing all year. As my counselor said, "You're not depressed. You're grieving as hard as you can." This is true. I have been grieving as hard and as thoroughly as I can. Feeling all of the emotions as they arise, mourning publicly, stepping into the pain, not aside from it. All because I am working towards a better life.

The first day of my grief class, we introduced ourselves. One of the ladies explained, "I lost my husband 10 years ago. I never dealt with it...so I am still dealing with it." I thought to myself, "You are the reason I am here. So I won't be you in 10 years."

From the very beginning of this journey, from the first month, I have been desperate to find a way out of the pain. For me, it wasn't about escape, though I grew to understand the lure of drugs, alcohol, sex, self-mutilation. I just couldn't take those escapes. I wanted them desperately, but I just couldn't do it. And at the end of the day, I knew that they wouldn't take me where I want to go.

I am grasping hard for a new life. It is not easy. It is one of the hardest things I've ever done. But there is no other option that is tenable. I can't go back. I refuse to stand still and spend the rest of my life trying to avoid this pain - and thereby living in it. There is only forward. That is the only choice.

Get busy living, or get busy dying. Right now, I am trying option one: get busy living.

Chapter 51

It's over

September 3, 2013

I just got the phone call from the lawyer's office. The court accepted our petition, and the estate is closed. I sit here on the couch listening to the warm, late summer rain and think, "Just like that. It's over." It's a quiet and gentle counterpoint to the violent accident that initiated this journey.

All his legal connections to this world have been snipped and neatly tied away. He is not coming back. Fuck. Have I told you lately how much I hate this? Death and the clean-up after? Each step is its own unique flavor of pain. I am tired of tasting them.

On my desk sit two stacks of paper. One is the legal paperwork from the estate. The other is a pile of cards, every single card I've received since the accident. Shortly after Mike's death, I decided the stacks would stay there until the estate was wrapped up. So...there they've lived for the year, growing slowly.

I don't know if they're supposed to be some sort of scale. Is the legal pain balanced by the cards of support and love? If that is the measure, the love clearly surpasses the pain.

The scale: legal versus love

Now, it is time to find another home for my piles. It is time to wrap them up and store them with other precious artifacts (the cards) and with other important papers (the legal side).

I am receiving a modest amount of money from the estate: reimbursement for the memorial reception and a fee for my time as the estate administrator. I prefer to think of it as a gift from Mike. I've been ruminating on how to spend it that would honor him.

When my grandparents passed, Mike suggested that I spend the inheritance on a motorcycle. Instead, I chose to put it towards my student loans, the option that my fiscally conservative grandparents would have appreciated.

Now, with what I am choosing to call my gift from Mike, I want to spend it in a way that is appropriate for him. It's not enough for a new motorcycle, but it's just about right to fund my upcoming solo motorcycle trip. To be honest, I'd prefer to purchase something tangible that I could hold on to in his memory, but spending it on this trip just feels right. And if I've learned anything in the past year, it's to trust my gut. Maybe through this trip, I will receive a gift more precious than anything I could purchase.

What I hope to find at the end of the road is...peace.

Part Two:
A Turning Point

September 2013

CHAPTER 52

Life after death: my first solo trip

This is the second – and longest – ride report, originally posted on the pnwriders.com and advrider.com motorcycle forums. It is edited here for brevity.

Drafted September 23, 2013 through October 13, 2013

Prelude:

Technically this ride began months ago. December 10th, to be exact. Well, possibly it began on August 22, 2012 when my boyfriend, Mike, died. But we'll settle on December 10th for this story. I was on a flight to California for work, reading Motorcycle Consumer News to pass the time, when I ran across this letter to the editor:

Ghost Rider

I enjoy your magazine and look forward to each issue arriving. Mark Barnes did a book review on "Ghost Rider" in the October 2012 issue, and I'm surprised at how he missed the point on this book.

There are many books that talk about motorcycle adventure and how to ride. There are few books that talk about riding a motorcycle as a way to avoid sending a bullet through your own brain. Neil's book does an amazing job of this.

If anyone you know or love has suffered the loss of a loved one, this book is a must-read.

Roland Cannon

Salt Lake City, UT

Immediately, I started crying. Averting my face to the window for some privacy on the full flight, I knew that I had to read this book. I downloaded it later that afternoon at the hotel.

Ghost Rider: Travels on the Healing Road was written by Neil Peart, the drummer from Rush. He lost his daughter in a car accident then his wife to cancer, all within the space of a year. He dealt with it by getting on his motorcycle and riding a total of 55,000 miles. Reading his story, I knew that someday I would do my own ride.

In March, my cousin sent me the book *Wild: From Lost to Found on the Pacific Crest Trail.* I devoured it in two days, laughing and crying along with the author, Cheryl Strayed, as she described her thousand miles of solo hiking to save herself after the loss of her mom. This book added to my determination to do my ride.

The urge to journey, to quest, to find some sort of redemption or resolution or peace...must be universal. Historically, the bereaved have journeyed solo to the mountains, the desert, and the sea. They have walked, cycled, backpacked...and motorcycled.

I have never received so many offers to travel as I did in the days and weeks after Mike's death. Friends and family invited me to New York, Florida, California, England, Brazil, and more.

But I knew that there was no use traveling until it was about moving forward, not escaping the past.

Last month was the one year anniversary of the accident. I've spent the year honoring him and, honestly, just trying to endure and survive. Stepping forward into the new year, the second year, I want it to be about moving forward, about choosing life.

This is my quest for life after death. I set off on my solo motorcycle trip September 10th and returned 10 days and 2,263 miles later.

The Preparation

I wondered how the trip would go. This trip meant setting off into the unknown in so many ways. Would I be lonely riding solo or sitting alone in restaurants and hotel rooms? Would I be able to handle the riding? What if I got lost, ran out of gas, had mechanical difficulties, or went down? Who would I meet on the road? Would people be threatening or helpful?

To be honest, I doubted that I had the riding skill or mechanical know-how to do a trip like this. But I wouldn't know until I tried. This past year, I've often felt like a burden on my friends, especially when it comes to motorcycling. I started from zero knowledge and needed to ask for help with every little thing. My amazing friends always generously helped me and shared their expertise. But eventually, I knew that I needed to learn how to do it on my own. I don't want to go through life being a leach.

The week before I departed, I did my first oil change and cleaned my chain, with step-by-step instruction from a friend. I was adamant that I wanted to do everything I could myself. Afterwards, he asked if this oil change was going on Facebook. I said yes but never posted it. Oddly, this oil change was too personal to put on Facebook. It was about claiming control over my own safety, about taking over the tasks that used to be Mike's, about facing my fears and inexperience doing anything mechanical. This minor maintenance task was major for me. It was the first step in my trip and aligned completely with my reasons for doing the trip. To see if I could do it on my own.

Preparation for the trip began in earnest a couple weeks before I left. I knew I should have started earlier but just felt on hold until the anniversary of the accident. Everything was in stasis until then. Afterwards, I threw myself into it: researched satellite communicators, picked up rain gear, considered GPS options, and vacillated over possible routes. I'm a researcher by trade, which can be a plus in some instances, but in this case, not so much. I was in a tizzy of preparation until the very last minute, when I finally forced myself out the door.

Planning

Packing

Bremerton, WA to Hood River, OR

Route: 268 miles: Bremerton, 16 south, I5 south, 512 east, 7 south (Morton), 12 east (Randle), FS 25, FS 90 (Cougar), FS 90, FS 51, FS 30 (Carson), 14 east, Hood River Bridge, 84 west, Columbia Cliff Villas Hotel in Hood River
Favorite road of the day: The new pavement on FS 30 into Carson.

I started the day harried and frantically trying to get out of town. It was a series of "just one last thing" until I set off, finally, at 1:00. With the last minute frustrations and feeling the daylight slipping away, I wasn't excited or nervous. I was just relieved to be on the road at last and felt pressure to keep moving.

All loaded up and ready to go!

Stopping in Morton for gas and a break, all of the parking spaces close to the mini mart were full so I slipped into a spot in front of the insurance agency across the lot. Crossing my fingers that they wouldn't mind me using one of their spots, I smiled at the ladies through the window. "Oh no," I thought with a sinking heart as one of them approached the door. "They're about to ask me to move." She poked her head out the door. "Do you need anything? Water? A bathroom?" Well...sure! I enjoyed their AC, a glass of cold water, and the use of their bathroom.

In exchange, they wanted to hear about me and my trip. Before the trip, a friend had told me that most people are kind to solo women riders and protective of them. This was my first time seeing it in action. They sent me off with smiles and reminders to be careful. I was humbled and heartened by their generosity. Full of good cheer and refreshed as much by their kindness as by the break, I continued on.

Parking in front of the insurance agency in Morton

As I rode farther into the countryside, the morning's tension flowed away. Winding through the base of Highway 25, I found myself saying, "Thank you, God, for the empty twisty roads, for the verdant hillsides, for the clear blue skies." I could breathe again.

Highway 25, Washington

It felt blissful to be riding alone. I reveled in the freedom to go my own pace and stop whenever I wanted...though, ever mindful of the passing sun, my breaks were short. I didn't know if I would enjoy riding alone throughout the trip, if this was just the "holiday" feel of setting off, but I enjoyed it for today.

Stopping for some photos, I longed to just sit and listen to the silence. The pressure to make it to the hotel before nightfall kept me moving, but I promised myself that sometime during this trip, I would find the space to listen to the silence of wilderness.

(When I was planning the route, it seemed more logical to take advantage of the good weather by traveling down the coast, but I just couldn't face the thought of joining the herd of tourists shuffling from one seaside town to the next. I longed for mountains and wilderness and solitude. I am glad I followed my heart. There is no question that these quiet, twisty roads fed my soul.)

Highway 25, Washington

As I continued on to Carson, dusk fell, and I was mindful of deer. Still, the fresh pavement beckoned, and I admit to having a little bit of fun on Highway 30. Riding along Highway 14 beside the Columbia River, night had fallen in earnest. The urgency to make Hood River before night had dissipated. It was already dark so why hurry? I enjoyed the warm night. It felt like I was swimming through currents of different temperature air, and the temps rose and fell by almost 10 degrees as the road twisted along the mountainside. I buzzed through the tunnels, and my headlight created a nimbus of light that followed my progress.

Crossing the bridge into Hood River, I felt a deep contentment. The view was gorgeous, with the mountains silhouetted against the last bit of orange sky. A crescent moon sliver hung above. I knew that I would make my goal for the day.

When I finally pulled into the hotel a little after 8:00, I was pleasantly surprised. It was a lovely, Spanish style hotel on the river. I had opted to splurge on the lodging for the first night, hoping that having a soft place to land at the end of the first day would make me feel better about traveling solo. I'm glad I did.

Columbia Cliff Villas Hotel, Hood River, Oregon

The only place walking distance for food was the historic hotel next door, the Columbia Gorge Hotel. When I arrived in the quiet, formal dining room, they first offered me a romantic table for two. It was set with linens and crystal, and I cringed at the idea of sitting there alone. With relief I spotted the bar in the next room. Luckily, they served food there, and I gratefully settled into the bar.

Beside the bar. I was bemused at finding myself in such a formal setting on a motorcycle trip. Very different from what I had pictured.

The bar was empty, except for one man working hard to pick up the bartender. She was moderately open to it and offered him her phone number, but the whole conversation seemed slightly sad and dreary. Is this what I have in store for me when I'm finally open to dating again? Sad conversations in empty bars? I tabled the thought for the future. There's nothing I can do about it now.

After heading back to my room, I started to run a bath in the deep soaker tub, only to find that the stopper wouldn't seal. With my newfound technical adventurousness, I took a look at the stopper. "Hmmm...I wonder if I can remove the spring?" With a little fiddling...ah ha! I disassembled it, sealed the tub, and enjoyed soaking my aches away.

With a full belly and relaxed from the bath, I climbed into the cozy bed and slept well. All in all, a successful first day. Maybe I could do this trip after all.

Hood River, OR to Oakridge, OR

Route: 237 miles: 35 south, 26 east, NF 42, NF 46, 22 east, 126 east then west (basically south), Cougar Dam Rd, Aufderheide Rd, 58 east, Best Western in Oakridge
Favorite roads of the day: NF 42 and NF 46

It was another beautiful day, and I took a moment to enjoy the view of the river before heading back to the Columbia Gorge Hotel for breakfast. As they sat me at the table for two, I looked up, and the empty seat before me seemed to be staring back. Something about the size and shape of the table reminded me forcefully of the last morning with Mike, sitting at a breakfast table in a different historic hotel planning our vacation, just hours before the accident. My throat tightened, and I surreptitiously wiped away some tears. I dutifully ate my yogurt parfait, listening to the next table loudly discuss their RV adventures.

The Columbia Gorge

Columbia Gorge Hotel dining room

My breakfast table

After loading the luggage, I again set off later than I wanted, about 10:00. The ride started off on Highway 35 through farm stands and self-pick orchards. The valley felt fresh and alive with growing produce. Mt. Hood was so clear and close that it was a little imposing, almost scary. The road wound up into the mountains along a river. It was fresh, cool, and pretty up there.

Check out that mountain!

Next, the ride became interesting, with what turned out to be my favorite roads of the day, NF 42 and 46. These roads

started off innocently enough but eventually became a beautifully maintained one lane road, very narrow with little pull outs.
This was one lane for real, no shoulder, and at the base of the
one lane portion was a "trucks" sign. Since I had passed a couple
logging trucks coming the opposite direction earlier, I sent a
hearty prayer not to find any on this road!

Oregon Skyline Road, NF 42, Oregon

Though it could have been scary, this ended up being my
favorite part of the day. It was warm and beautiful up there, with
wildflowers lining the road. It felt like an adventure. I'd stop at
each intersection and consult my GPS and written directions.
Along the way, I found wooden signs pointing to the Pacific
Crest Trail, which made me feel close to the author of the book,
Wild, and her journey of loss and redemption. This would have
been a perfect place to sit and listen to the silence, but again, I
needed to keep tootling along if I was going to make it to my
hotel by nightfall. (Yes, I recognize the start of a pattern here.)

NF 46. This was a pull-out so it was wider than the real road, which you can see ahead.

With some regret, I bid farewell to the wilderness and turned onto Highway 22, a forested two lane highway. Still, while I was sad to say goodbye to the wilderness, there were more roads before me to discover!

The heat rose as I descended the mountain, and I continued

on in temps up to 96 degrees. All of a sudden, I had a moment of clarity. I realized that I was getting increasingly impatient with the traffic ahead because I was desperate to find the turnoff to Aufderheide Road and ascend to cooler temps.

This was silly and dangerous. I needed to cool down now, not by pushing ahead. I found a gas station and went inside to cool off. I plopped down in the shade outside with my two cold bottles of water, patiently struggled out of my jacket, and slowly returned to a functioning temperature.

As I sat there leaning against the wood siding of the building, drinking my cold water, a grizzled hippy looking man stopped to talk to me. It started with him admiring the bike and telling me he doesn't like to go too fast. He had picked up a six-pack at the store and invited me back to his house for a beer. "I'm harmless," he said with a laugh, "and single!" His eyes alit as he turned to me. "Oh, I forgot to ask!" With a gesture at the bikes, he interrupted himself, "Well, there's only one bike."

I sat on the sidewalk and silently surveyed my bike. I felt the lack of a second bike acutely. Mike should have been here with me. I responded haltingly, "Well, this isn't exactly a memorial ride, but my boyfriend died last year so...this trip is to deal with that. So, yes, I guess I am single." Single. The word tasted ugly and strange in my mouth. I think this was actually the first time I uttered the phrase "I am single." I looked at him with tears in my eyes.

It surprises me how often this happens, but when I share my loss, people often share theirs as well. This man had lost 12 people in the past five years. As we wrapped up the conversation, he didn't give up on the invitations. "I have a house, on a creek, on 10 acres! It's just back there! You could follow me, easy!" His banter put a smile on my face as he drove off in his old beater pickup.

I was cooled down now, and as I threw on my neck cooler and set off again, I was excited. Aufderheide. The whole reason I had picked this day's route was to ride this road. I've heard good things about it, and I had been disappointed that we didn't get to ride it on the memorial ride. As I climbed into the mountains, for the first time I deeply missed riding with Mike's friends. I could picture them cutting through the turns before me with a gentle grace belying the power and speed of their machines.

I was surprised by the dam. It was beautiful! I stopped and jumped off my bike to take pics, sweat dripping down my face into the helmet padding. I then continued on in my slow, careful way. The road was pretty beat up in places, with a lot of debris and one full gravel washboard section. Gravel is my nemesis so I was glad to see that it wasn't long.

Cougar Dam, Oregon

Aufderheide Road., Oregon

At my first stop sign back in civilization, it was a treat to find a beautiful covered bridge. I didn't have enough guts to stop on the bridge for pics so I just pulled over at the stop sign and snapped away.

Office Covered Bridge, Westfir, Oregon

Office Covered Bridge, Westfir, Oregon

From there, it was only a short distance to the Best Western in Oakridge. I didn't sleep as well this night and woke from 3:30 to 4:45 am. In the middle of the night, I felt very alone and lost, in a random motel room, in a random town in the middle of Oregon. I pictured how it would have been if Mike was asleep beside me and hugged a pillow. Eventually, I slipped back into slumber until morning, when I awoke ready for more adventure.

Oakridge, OR to Grants Pass, OR

Route: 228 miles: 58 east, 97 south, 138 west, Crater Lake North Highway, Rim Drive, Munson Valley Road, 62 west, 234 west, Meadows Road, Evans Creek Road, I5 north, La Quinta in Grants Pass
Favorite roads of the day: Meadows and Evans Creek

The day dawned bright and sunny, and I felt like I was starting to get into the swing of the trip. After a quick bowl of cereal at the hotel breakfast, I loaded up the bike. Climbing on, my first thought was, "Well, what interesting roads are we going to find today?" I was happy to be on the bike and moving.

To tell the truth, I didn't expect much from the roads today. The focus of the day was Crater Lake, and I had forgone the interesting roads to visit this sight. As I plugged the waypoints into the GPS, it offered three alternative routes. One of them showed an alluring back roads route. Hmmm...try it or not? I was well aware of the tragic outcomes possible from blindly following a GPS, but it sure was tempting.... With a sigh, I opted for the standard highway route and hit the road.

A while later, I took a break on Highway 58. I snapped a

couple pics, had a bite of a granola bar and reconsidered that tempting off-highway route. The experience on NF 42 and 46 had given me a taste of back roads, and I wanted more. Surely, it couldn't hurt to just try this route. I doubted that it would go through, but wouldn't it be lovely if it did? (Note that I had the GPS set to avoid unpaved roads. I was looking for off-highway, not off-road.)

Feeling audacious, I threw caution to the wind and hit "Go" on the off-highway route. Now I was having an adventure! I recalled the days not so long ago – just last year, in fact – when I'd only ride two carefully planned loops close to home.

Happy, I rolled along. The GPS told me to turn on 429. "This is it!" It was a two-lane country road that soon crossed into national forest land. I felt bright, awake, and curious. The GPS told me to turn, and suddenly, the road surface became gravel. I slowed to a crawl as I saw that the road had turned to dirt and had wooden bollocks across it. "Huh, the GPS wants me to take what looks like a trail?" Shrug. "Oh well, this is the end of the line for me." I knew it was unlikely that this route would work out, but my mini adventure-exploration was fun. I pulled into the gravel parking lot for the beach beside me, took a couple photos, and headed back the way I came.

My detour: South Simax Beach, Oregon

Back on 58, I knew that I had "wasted" enough time, and it was time to put some miles behind me. I was curious about Crater Lake. I remembered Mike's photos from his solo ride in 2008. They were stunning – the red Aprilia RSVR before the crystal blue lake. I wanted to see it for myself. Soon enough, I was pulling into the park.

The North Entrance Road climbed up to the crater, and eventually, I saw a parking lot with a few cars at Merriam Point. This was it! I parked and hiked up the small hill for my first glimpse of the lake. With this much build-up, I expected to be walloped by the sight, but...that just didn't happen. It certainly wasn't your average lake, but I wasn't overwhelmed either. A few clouds had gathered over the lake, and the small ripples reflecting them gave the view an otherworldly feel. Oddly, I was probably more disappointed in my reaction than in the lake itself. Maybe there was a better view along the crater that would prompt a better reaction?

My first view of Crater Lake, Oregon

Wicked helmet hair and Crater Lake

Returning to the parking area, I found that my bike had made a friend. Another bike was parked beside it, and I met Paul, who was on his way back home to San Diego. We wished each other safe travels, and I continued on.

I stopped several times for the obligatory "bike in front of the lake" photos but never did find the view to prompt an "oh wow" response. You just can't force a religious experience. I had thought that with the extra time in my schedule today, I might spend some quiet time here at the lake, but no, this wasn't the place for it.

Obligatory 'bike and Crater Lake' photo

At the Rim Village, I stopped for lunch. Juggling tuna salad, coffee, helmet, and tank bag, I settled into an outside table. It was fun to eavesdrop on all the different languages and accents: German, French, and several British accents surrounded me. Soon enough, I heard an American accent, "Mind if I join you?"

It was Paul, and I was happy to have some lunchtime company. We shared stories from the road, and he explained that he had originally wanted to ride to Alaska but not any longer. He didn't want to have to traverse the length of California again. He had already done it once on the way up and now was doing it again on the way home.

You'll probably laugh at me, but this was the first time that it occurred to me that I was going to have to ride home. My focus had been very day-by-day or even road-by-road. But I was now struck with the uncomfortable thought that every mile I rode was a commitment to ride the same distance back. I tried not to think about it, but this disquieting nugget was lodged in the back of my brain. I bid Paul goodbye once again and headed out of the park.

Descending from the crater, I noticed that I was riding poorly. I was uncomfortable on the bike. This puzzled me. What was going on? I realized that I was afraid – not of anything in particular, but my body was full of fear. Who did I think I was to attempt to ride so far? And then I would have to ride all the way home. What if the weather turned? What if? What if? I rode through the fear. It didn't occur to me to turn back. Riding through the fear is what this year's been about. Over and over again, stepping into the fear.

As I descended, the green, tree-lined rural highway began to leach some of the fear away. The temps rose and rose to the mid-90s, and the heat boiled the fear out of my blood, melted it out of my bones. I relaxed into the ride. There is no use worrying about tomorrow. There is only now, the warm haze, and the unrolling road.

In the late afternoon/early evening, the sun spread long, golden rays across the landscape. I figured I was in the home stretch to the hotel and had made peace with the unexciting route of the day. It was still a lovely day.

This is when the GPS told me to turn onto Meadows Road, and I found my bliss. A beautiful, freshly paved two-lane road, deserted, gently winding over hills and along rivers. It was not wilderness; there were driveways and fences, yet the houses were tucked away and not visible from the road. It felt solitary. I was overwhelmed with gratitude for this moment. Meadows Road led to Evans Creek Road, and the beauty continued.

Meadow's Road, Oregon

Eventually, it was time to jump on I5 for a short while, the last stretch to Grants Pass. Merging on, I looked in the mirror and squeaked out, "Oh shit!" as I grabbed the brakes. A big rig barreling towards me passed, and passed, and passed. It was a triple trailer. We don't have those in my neck of the woods.

Scary. I stayed in the slow lane and was glad when it was time to exit.

Riding through Grants Pass, the smoke from the forest fires to the south looked ominous in the setting sun. I'd need to decide tomorrow morning whether to change my route to avoid the fires.

Wildfire smoke visible from Grants Pass, Oregon

I pulled into the La Quinta a little after dark and settled into the room with dinner and laundry, feeling unexpectedly homey. It had been a good day, though the most enjoyable parts were completely different than I had expected. I noticed that this was a trend and reminded myself to keep an open mind and enjoy the moment throughout the trip. I tucked myself in for a good night's sleep.

Grants Pass, OR to Fortuna, CA

Route: 223 miles: 199 south (Cave Junction), NF 48 south (Happy Camp), 96 south (Willow Creek), 299 west (Arcata), 101 south, Comfort Inn in Fortuna
Favorite roads of the day: NF 48 and the S-curves at the base of 96

The morning started with a serious call home to my mom to discuss routing options. I needed a second opinion. We sat on the phone, both looking at various websites, trying to figure out the severity of the wildfires and the impact on the roads. I had been looking forward to these roads for months – the highlight of my trip – but I also had a healthy respect for wildfires. Riding alone into a forest with an uncontrolled fire wouldn't be smart. Looking at the official websites, it appeared that the wildfires were at least 80% contained and not too close to my route. The Caltrans site showed no road closures due to fire, though they did say that delays were possible on Highway 96. I decided to give it a shot.

I set off on 199 and took a break in Cave Junction. I stopped at a gas station and pulled out my map. This is where I met

Wayne, a retired truck driver. He was on his cell phone, sitting on the swing beside the espresso stand. "Give me the map," he barked at me. Uh...okay. I handed over the map thinking that I could always buy another one if he didn't give it back. But we started to talk, and I could see that he wasn't being rude. He just had a brusque, straightforward manner of speaking. "It's good to see a lady on the road," he said. His Harley was parked in the shade. We talked routes, and he offered to show me the way to NF 48. Cool!

Now, don't worry, I wouldn't ride blindly off with another rider. My GPS was on, and the GPS lady's cool British voice narrated each turn before he took it. It was fun to ride with someone else, even though it was only for about 10 minutes. We must have made a funny looking pair – him with his ape hanger handlebars, tank top, and skull cap helmet and me in my leathers on my oddball bike. We reached the "four corners" stop sign, and he pointed left for 48 to Happy Camp. "Thank you!" I yelled to him through my helmet with a big grin.

I loved NF 48. I'm not a fast rider so I wasn't blazing along. But I was happy as a clam tooling along at my own mellow pace. It was deserted; I think only one car passed the whole way to Happy Camp. Nice clean pavement, beautiful forest, twisty. Soon after starting off, I realized that I was having difficulty trail braking. Before I left for the trip, I had asked a friend to help adjust the brake lever, and now it was just too hard to reach. Well, there's no time like the present to learn how to do it myself!

I pulled over and dug out the torx wrench. I had seen it adjusted twice but never done it myself. It made me laugh that the first time I adjusted it would be alone on the side of a deserted,

remote road in the forest. As flippant as I seem now, I was me-
thodical at the time, well aware that if I messed up, I'd be stuck.
Brakes are kind of a necessity. The adjustment went fine, and I
was back on the road quickly.

Roadside lever adjustments on NF 48, Oregon

Soon enough, I saw the "Welcome: Heart of Klamath" sign and knew I had arrived in Happy Camp. I breathed a sigh of relief, and a feeling of elation suffused me. Wow. I actually made it to California. Who would have thought? Certainly not me. All winter long, I had been talking about doing a road trip to California in September, but I never actually believed it. Regardless of the proof surrounding me, I was still in disbelief. Of course, photos were a necessity, both here and at the giant bigfoot statue.

Happy Camp. I made it to California.

I stopped at a pizza place, ordered a chicken fajita sandwich (yummy), and plopped down in a booth directly in front of the AC. I was enjoying my lunch when a text came through from my best friend. It was a photo of her with her newborn daughter, born just that morning. My heart squeezed tightly, and I set my food aside. You know how some babies just look like baby-shaped lumps? That wasn't the case here. This baby girl was beautiful. Her eyes were closed, and her fist was in her mouth. I loved her already. My heart felt bruised.

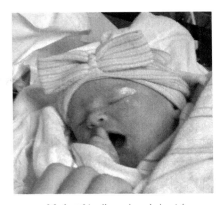

My best friend's newborn baby girl

I looked up to see my bike through the window, and it seemed so strange how the choices you make in life can bring you to unexpected crossroads. We started out in the same high school. Here I was alone on a motorcycle in a small town, while she just gave birth to her third child. I looked at that photo and knew that I was unlikely to have children. That was one of the losses with Mike. I'm okay with it in the abstract, but looking at the photo...well, it did make me wonder.

Happy Camp, California

After sending a note of congratulations, it was time to keep moving. I was nicely chilled from the AC, but as I geared up, I noticed that I had left my earplugs in the tank bag in the heat. Inserting them felt like pouring molten wax in my ears, heating my brain. Yuck! Note to self, take earplugs inside during breaks.

Next up, Highway 96. I'd been looking forward to this road, as it came highly recommended by Mike and his friends. They had all enjoyed it during their road trip a few years ago.

About 10 minutes out of town, I came around a corner to find a motorcycle in the ditch. I quickly scanned the situation. Two riders were struggling to right the bike; one rider was walking on the other side of the road. Everyone still had their helmets on so this must have just happened. I didn't see anyone lying down so hopefully everyone was okay.

As I pulled to the side of the road, I wondered if this was the right thing to do. I know that you're not supposed to crowd accident sites. Still, I was carrying a first aid kit and some tools so maybe I could help. As I turned off my bike, another rider who had been traveling in the other direction did a U-turn and parked behind me. Another couple riders traveling separately parked on the other side.

The rider who had gone down was walking around the accident site swearing in his helmet. I figured that was a good sign, though adrenaline can mask a lot. Eventually, everyone took their helmets off, and we assessed the situation. It turned out that the rider was fine, though his bike was seriously damaged, and it had left a pool of oil in the road. Once it was clear that everyone was okay, I snapped some pictures.

The damaged bike, Highway 96, California

We all introduced ourselves and learned a bit about each other. The guy who had pulled up behind me was on his way back to Portland. He asked about my route. "So, did you just take I5?" "Oh no," I responded. He ran down the list of highways. "101? 97?" I kept shaking my head. As I explained my route, his eyes got bigger and bigger. "Wow, you're really doing it!" His response made me feel good. Hey, maybe I'm really doing it. Little did he know that I'd be way more intimidated to ride that far on I5 than back roads.

You would think that coming across a group of guys on a road trip having had an accident would hit me like a gut punch. It did make me think but not like a gut punch. Oddly, what I mainly felt was a combination of relief that everyone was okay and mild irritation that the rider wouldn't stop complaining. Didn't he know how lucky he was? His friends could have been standing there frantically trying to save him. They could have been standing there having lost him. They were all so lucky. This was just a typical, semi-mundane accident and not a tragedy. They didn't seem to realize the bullet that they had dodged. For them, this was a disappointment on their road trip. For me, it was a tragedy averted. I didn't blame them for not seeing things the same way as me. This is just one of the ways I'm different than others since Mike's accident.

We stood around on the side of the road until it looked like everything was under control. As I was getting ready to set off again, one of the other riders in the group said to me, "I just have two words for you: BE. CAREFUL."

"I am," I replied. "My boyfriend died last year in a motorcycle accident while on a road trip with his friends...so I definitely understand." He looked shocked and somber. "I'm sorry," he said. "It's okay," I replied. "It's hard, but you have to keep moving ahead," I said, gesturing at the road.

The road ahead, Highway 96, California

It felt good to be moving. I was relieved to find that I was still happy to be on the road. Coming across the accident hadn't given me second thoughts about my trip.

The heat affected me much worse today. It was probably a combination of being dehydrated and not being able to eat enough the past few days, but I just wasn't making the progress that I wanted. I stopped several times to cool down, but by the time I reached Willow Creek at the junction of 96 and 299, I knew I'd have to change my route.

Taking a break in Willow Creek, California

Originally, I had wanted to take 299 east from here, 3 south, and 36 west to Fortuna. But it was 3:30, and the past few days had shown me that 1) everything took me longer than I expected and 2) finishing the day riding into the sun wasn't fun. I scrapped my ambitious route and begrudgingly turned towards the coast. The revised route was 299 west to 101 south.

Highway 299 came highly recommended, and I had been looking forward to it, but I found it a bit nerve wracking. The problem was the traffic. I didn't relish passing big rigs in corners with big rigs and RV's in the oncoming lane, especially as it was not a divided highway. When I came around a corner and saw a giant, dark wall of fog ahead, all I wanted to do was turn around and run back to the sunny hills. The temps dropped and dropped, from low 90's to low 60's, and I pulled off at the empty truck scales to add some layers.

Now in the heavy, low cloud bank, I merged onto 101. I had picked Fortuna as a destination so I could skip Eureka, but this revised route led me down the length of Eureka in rush hour traffic. It was gray skies, gray roads, gray sea, tons of traffic, lots of cops, multiple stop lights, a center turn lane with left-turners, and bunches of little side streets that squirted cars out into the main thoroughfare. Creeping along with traffic near the waterfront, I was overwhelmed by the smell of trash and decomposing fish. "Oh my God, what is that SMELL?!" I said aloud in my helmet before holding my breath. The wilderness of the morning seemed long ago and far away.

I rode with my shoulders scrunched up and a dour look on my face. But I had to laugh when the image popped into my head of a cat that had just gotten a bath. You know that slightly offended look they have? That's about how I looked riding through Eureka.

I pulled up to the Comfort Inn in Fortuna glad to call it a day. As I was checking in, the man behind me in line interrupted. "Excuse me, but were you at Crater Lake yesterday?" "No," I blurted out. "Oh wait, yes!" Crater Lake was just yesterday? Standing in this cold seaside town, it felt like ages ago. It turned out that this couple had sat next to me during lunch at Crater Lake. They were one of the tables of British accents. It sure is a small world.

After checking in, I asked the attendant if there was anything in walking distance for dinner. When he mentioned the Eel River Brewery across the parking lot, my outlook immediately took a turn for the better. Score! I changed and walked to the brewery.

Eel River Brewery, Fortuna, California

Sitting in their patio, I noticed that the couple at the next table was wearing black leather jackets and heavy leather boots. Taking a chance, I asked if they were motorcycle riders. It turns out that they were, and we had a nice conversation over dinner, sharing stories from the road. It's interesting. Though I'm traveling alone, I feel part of a far-flung family of motorcyclists. Everywhere I go, whether I know them or not, I can be assured of a friendly reception from other motorcyclists on the road. It's comforting.

Fortuna, CA to Willits, CA

Route: 159 miles:101 south, Avenue of the Giants, 101 south, 1 south (Fort Bragg), 20 east (Willits), Super 8 in Willits
Favorite road of the day: Hwy 20

I started off the day tying myself in knots about which way to go. For lack of a better plan, my original goal for the trip was to travel as far south as the Nepenthe Restaurant in Big Sur. This plan had a number of advantages. I had grown up in the Bay Area so traveling there meant that I could visit family, meet my best friend's new daughter, hold a meeting with some clients in Monterey (aka write off the trip), and have the chance to ride some familiar roads for the first time, since I didn't learn to ride until moving away.

But down deep I fundamentally did not want to ride in the Bay Area: too much traffic, and I had traveled those roads before. There would be no exploration or discovery. My heart quailed at the thought of riding through the congestion of San Francisco. And finally, that niggling doubt about the weather changing had never left me. In the Pacific Northwest, the end of September is chancy weather-wise. I could be signing myself up for the whole return trip in the rain. I'm not a fair weather rider, but 1,000+ miles of rain riding wouldn't be fun.

I wrestled with whether cutting out the southern portion of the trip would signify conceding to my fears. Whether it would disappoint my family and friends. I called a friend and talked it out. Ultimately, I decided that this trip was for me. What I really wanted was more time on those gorgeous northern California roads. That is what felt healing to me. At this point in the trip, I knew that I *could* ride through the congestion of the Bay Area, but why do it if I didn't want to? I decided to travel south today, and that would be as far south as I would go. From there, I would work my way north, spending some extra time in northern California. As soon as I made this decision, the tension eased in my chest.

The first destination of the day was the Avenue of the Giants. I grew up in a redwood forest so it felt like home riding through the redwood trees, like visiting friends. The Avenue is just a small, two-lane road, often straight, except where it curves around trees. The attraction here is the sights, not the road itself.

I had read about the Founders Circle in Destination Highways so I pulled off there to do the half mile "hike". I was crossing the road to start the hike when I heard a small bike and turned to see a little scooter loaded down with traveling and camping gear. This guy obviously had a story!

The forest was beautiful, and it was fun to get off the bike and explore a bit. Trying to take self portraits in front of giant trees is not easy. I played with different angles and laughed as I tried to run to beat the three-second timer on the cell phone camera.

Halfway through the walk, another solo traveler asked me to take a photo of him, and it turned out to be the guy on the scooter. Alex was German, and he was on his way from Vancouver to Argentina. He was 10 weeks into his 18 month trip. We finished the walk together gabbing about adventures and snapping photos, then compared bikes and wished each other well.

Founders' Grove Nature Loop Trail, Humboldt Redwoods State Park, California

The Founders' Tree (361' tall, 40' circumference), Humboldt Redwoods State Park, California

Next up, Highway 1! Now, let me preface this by sharing that my main other experience with Highway 1 was between Santa Cruz and Carmel, a pretty but well-traveled, straight coastal highway. I set off assuming that Highway 1 would be the touristy part of my trip. I thoroughly – shall we say vastly – under-estimated this road. It was completely remote and the longest stretch of tight, TIGHT twisties that I've ever encountered, roughly 25 miles. It was the first road of the trip where I thought they actually overestimated the speed on the corner signs. I traversed almost the entire 25 miles in first gear, a humbling experience.

When I finally reached the coast, I pulled over for a well deserved break. The guardrail was covered with interesting graffiti, kind of like a sign-in book for visitors. I took photos of some that caught my eye then felt moved to add my own. I grabbed my ballpoint pen and in the top of one of the wooden supports wrote, "RIP Mike. I love you. 9/14/13." My heart clenched, and I breathed deeply of the sea air. I wondered if he had ever ridden through here. If so, he had probably stopped at this pull-out, the first after the twisty section, and stared out over this same ocean. I pictured other visitors after me reading my words and wondering the story behind them, as I wondered the story behind the other inscriptions.

First sight of the California coast. Highway 1

My roadside graffiti, Highway 1, California

The highway wound along the coast, and while I was glad to have gotten some coastal experience in this trip, I was also relieved not to be doing the coast all the way down to Big Sur. It was gray and chilly. Pretty...but rather glum.

I finally rolled into Fort Bragg just before 3:00 and stopped for a late lunch, where I ate and surfed the options for lodging. I booked the Super 8 in Willits and headed for Highway 20. What an unexpected treasure of a road! Beautifully maintained, two lanes with lots of pull-outs, it wound through the forest. The curves were tight enough to keep my interest without being so tight they were punishing.

All through Highway 1, I had felt that I wasn't riding well. I have difficulty being smooth on the really tight, technical roads. I'd found myself stiffly pushing the bike down beneath me. "Candiya, don't ride like a doofus. You know better than that," I'd admonished myself, to no effect. But on Highway 20, I finally started to loosen up. What a fun ride to Willits. And sunny – yay! It was definitely the right choice to come this way. I felt my spirit lightening.

For dinner, I asked the front desk clerk what was in walking distance. He pointed down 101 and named several restaurants. I started walking but was not impressed with the atmosphere of the neighborhood.

Before I left on the trip, several friends had offered to teach me how to shoot in case I wanted to bring a gun. Others said that situational awareness would keep me safe. In the end, I was too overwhelmed with the preparations to think about guns so I opted to rely on situational awareness. This meant that I had to actually pay attention and not discount any misgivings.

I didn't feel totally safe walking this road at dusk. There was little foot traffic – a couple homeless men, a pretty normal looking guy, and an "interesting" guy walking with a staff as tall as his head. I decided to stop at the first restaurant I saw. I walked in and almost immediately walked out because it didn't smell very good. But the waitress greeted me with a bright smile so I sat down and perused the menu.

You know you're concerned when you're reviewing the menu looking for the items least likely to make you sick. The food was awful – some of the worst I've ever had. I ate the salad but left 85% of the entree. By then it was dark, and I still needed to walk back. I figured that I had eaten a good lunch, and I'd eat a good breakfast in the morning. I could skip dinner. The walk home was fast and quiet. I was happy to get back to the safe haven of the hotel.

Willits, CA to McCloud, CA

Route: 311 miles: 101 north (Garberville), Alderpoint Road, 36 east, 3 north, 299 east (Redding), I5 north (Dunsmuir), 89 east, McCloud River Mercantile Hotel in McCloud
Favorite roads of the day: Alderpoint Rd. and Hwy 36

In the morning, I sat down to do some route planning with my maps, GPS, and the Destination Highways app. I was like a kid in a candy store picking out my treats. "I'll take one of these and one of those." I added one fun road after another to the route. It felt delicious. This is the gift I had given myself with the decision to cut out the southern portion of the trip.

The big question was where to end for the day. I followed Highway 3 north on the map and found Weed. Looking at lodging options there, some bed and breakfasts popped up in McCloud. When I started the trip, I'd had a vague idea about staying in a B&B at the coast, but that hadn't happened. Maybe this could be my chance. I found one with excellent reviews and a mention of a soaker tub. Sold! I booked it. The only small doubt I had was the review that mentioned that no restaurants were open for dinner in walking distance. "Oh well," I thought, picturing a B&B in the middle of a forest. I'd deal with that when I arrived.

The other question was if I could cut from Highway 101 to Highway 36 without returning all the way to Fortuna. There were some small lines on the map that looked like they'd go through, but were those roads paved? I tried putting them in the GPS with the "avoid unpaved" option set, curious if it would work. The GPS accepted the route without a hiccup. Cool! We'll give it a shot.

Route set, I was excited to get on the road, but I needed to eat first after skipping dinner last night. Looking at the hotel breakfast buffet of processed food options, I settled on the instant oatmeal. Oatmeal's healthy, right? Unfortunately, it was so sweet, I could only choke down about half of it before giving up. The road beckoned! I'd eat a good lunch on the way.

I set off and found 101 to be unexpectedly pleasant, winding through the forest with minimal traffic. Soon, I was at Garberville. I got gas and contemplated heading into town for lunch since it was 11:00, but I wasn't ready to stop yet. "There will be something else up the road."

So...on to Alderpoint Road! Other than my short detour on the way to Crater Lake, this was my first non-highway road that didn't come with a firsthand recommendation from someone on the motorcycle forum or the Destination Highways book. I knew this was taking a chance, which is why I stopped for gas before setting off. Now, this was exploration!

The road set off with fairly good pavement and gorgeous views. I stopped to take some photos before a 10 mph hairpin, then again a bit later. Sitting on the shoulder, I noticed that every vehicle that passed was four-wheel drive, and the only motorcycle I saw was a dual sport. I wondered if this presaged anything about the road conditions ahead.

Alderpoint Road above Garberville, California

The road wound along, and the pavement deteriorated further and further. This was truly the nastiest pavement I've ever come across. It didn't just have frost heaves, it had buckles and ridges and potholes, sometimes all atop one another. I loved it, just ate it up, motoring along slowly, wondering what was around the next bend. The road narrowed to one lane, and I continued to wonder. I passed a sign that said loose gravel. There was a stop sign, then a single lane of gravel for about 20 feet. The sign said to proceed when clear. I carefully rode across at minimal speed, with my foot hovering over the rear brake. Onward!

I continued on, around and over hills, until I came to another loose gravel sign. I looked for a stop sign, any sort of indication that this was a defined section of gravel, but there wasn't one. The pavement just...ended. I could see the two lane gravel road go up over the crown of a hill and around the bend.

I was ready for a break so I turned off my bike, took off my helmet, and broke out a health bar. It was now getting on towards 12:30 with no lunch in sight. Okay...how to proceed? I checked my gas: 70 miles on the tank. I figured that this was about the halfway mark on the tank so if I was going to turn back, I should do it now. I looked at the GPS: about 26 more miles to Highway 36. Was there more pavement up ahead or 26 miles of gravel that might deteriorate into something that required the four-wheel capability of all the pickups that had passed me earlier? I stood there in the warm summer day, munching my bar, dodging the bees that were fascinated with my bike, and pondered. "I sure wish I could ask someone..."

Gravel ahead...

And pavement behind

"Wait, what's that sound?" Over the buzzing bees and hum of the power lines, I heard the rumble of a motor, and then it faded away. Hmmm... I munched and listened and sure enough, the sound of the motor returned, even closer. Hell yeah.

Over the crown of the gravel hill, I saw a rental sedan with an older couple in it, followed by yet another four-wheel drive truck. I was irrationally relieved to see that sedan, the first non-four-wheel-drive vehicle of the road. "If they can make it through, so can I!" I flagged them down with a grin.

"How much farther does the gravel go?" I asked them.

"Oh, not far, maybe a half mile," they answered.

"And then it's paved from then on?"

"Well, there are a few spots of gravel, but this is the longest," they replied.

"And this road connects with 36?" It seemed wise to double check.

"Yes," they confirmed.

I thanked them with a smile and gave a wave to the poor pickup truck, stuck behind the rental car. Woot! I was back in business.

Crossing that boundary from paved to unpaved was important. I couldn't believe that I was doing this, and even moreso, I couldn't believe that I was *excited* to do this. Who was I? Surely I was not the same person who struggled with debilitating nerves while learning to ride, the person who wanted everything planned and under control. No, the truth is that I am not that person anymore. Since Mike's accident I have not held any expectation that I would be the same person as before. But I didn't know that I had changed in this way. I didn't know that I was strong and adventurous. I didn't know that I could relish the challenge of the unknown.

Crunching across the gravel, I thought ruefully that this was probably not what my friends meant when they had told me to be careful. I was going to get a "talking to" when they found out about this. Continuing forward was a commitment to face the unknown since I probably didn't have enough gas to retrace my steps. I was on a quiet rural road of uncertain condition. No one knew where I was, though I had set my satellite communicator to place a dot on an online map each hour. I had some backup in the form of the communicator, but in the immediate short-term, I needed to rely on myself. And that was okay.

I continued on and on. There were probably six to seven small sections of gravel. Gravel with washboard ruts...ba-bump, ba-bump...gravel on top of mud...uphill gravel and downhill gravel. My confidence improved with each crossing, and my hesitation before each attempt shortened and shortened until there was no hesitation.

The road opened up to a gorgeous view. By now it was 1:30,

time for another break. I pulled over, walked across the road, and settled my bum on the berm with a bottle of water and another granola bar. Since the first day of my trip, I had been wanting to sit and listen to the silence, and I decided that I wasn't going to let this opportunity slip through my fingers. I closed my eyes. All I could hear was the buzzing of bees and the shhhhh... of the tall dry grass stalks rubbing in the slight breeze. I opened my eyes and watched the grass bounce and wave before me. The individual stalks bent in ripples, as if the field was a single organism. My eye scanned the horizon, following the dry hillside to find a single tree silhouetted against the sky and the darker tree-covered hills in the distance. The air was warm and smelled like the dusty end of summer. Eventually, I knew it was time to move along. More interesting roads awaited.

Alderpoint Road, California

Do you see the solitary tree in the distance?

Can you hear the rustle of the grass?

I continued on and soon saw the GPS read that Highway 36 was within a mile. I knew then that I was going to make it and felt a triumphant rush. I purred along over the last gravel section with nary a flutter of hesitation. I've never been as excited to see a stop sign as I was when I reached HIghway 36.

Highway 36 was a surprise. I don't know why, but with its exalted reputation in the motorcycling community, I figured it would be a main thoroughfare. I pictured it as two lanes in each direction with steady traffic. Instead, I was at a deserted intersection. The highway stretched across with only one lane in each direction, and it was empty. I sat there for a minute...still empty. As I turned right onto the highway and accelerated on the fresh, new pavement, the thought rang in my head, "I am in heaven!" It was glorious. The difference from the past three hours of broken pavement could not have been more absolute. This road was amazing. Amazing!

And as an extra gift, I quickly realized that at my skill level, I could go as fast as I wanted, and I was still going the speed limit. Bonus! I passed three parked police cars, and I'm sure the officers were shaking their heads at me, hanging off the bike at the speed limit. (Yes, I know there's no need to hang off at the speed limit, but I was playing and practicing. After conquering Alderpoint, I deserved a little play!)

Of course, I had once again underestimated the remoteness of these roads. I kept a look-out for gas and stopped at the first station I came across. Pulling into the station, I looked at my trip meter, which said that I had about 70 miles on the tank. Wait a minute, wasn't it 70 miles when I stopped at the beginning of the gravel? Embarrassed, I realized that I hadn't waited for the bike to cycle through its readouts when I looked at the screen on Alderpoint. It was 70 degrees then, not 70 miles. Oops. Well, better to have extra in reserve than the opposite.

Usually, at gas stations, people were curious or encouraging. This gas station was a strange place. The men lounged against the walls and looked at me with hard eyes. I pumped the gas and got out of there as quickly as possible.

Soon, it was time to turn onto Highway 3. This was a fun road too, though tighter than Highway 36. I knew that my skills weren't doing it justice. I should have been able to go faster, but all I could do was continue on in my comfort zone.

It was getting on towards 3:00 when I hit Hayfork. I still hadn't eaten so I stopped at the market for a bottle of water and a package of six cheese-filled crackers. As I downed them as quickly as possible in the parking lot, the lady behind the register came outside to tell me that there was a lot of gravel on Highway 3 and to be careful. More kindness from strangers.

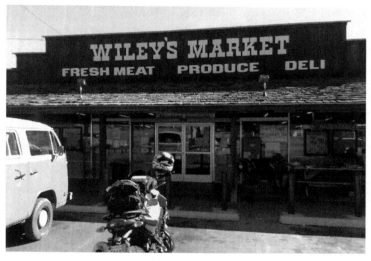

The market in Hayfork, California

As I gassed up in Hayfork, I had to admit that there wasn't enough daylight left to complete the rest of my route so I changed my plan. Now I'd take 299 to Redding and I5 north. Though I had to cut my route short, I couldn't begrudge the day. What I had already experienced was amazing. Highway 299 was fun, though it became busier approaching Redding. This was the biggest city I'd been in since leaving the Seattle area, and I noticed that I was much more comfortable than I typically was riding in traffic.

This day of riding put a smile on my face. Highway 299, outside Redding, California

As I approached I5, I sent a fervent prayer..."Please be kind, I5!" I was deathly afraid of riding on I5 in the Seattle area. I knew it was likely to be less congested here, but still, the thought of spending 55 miles on it wasn't pleasant. With a bunch of pent-up tension, I merged on to the freeway...to find it almost deserted. The nearest vehicles were about a half mile ahead and a half mile behind me. I let out a giant sigh of relief. This was excellent freeway practice. I was on the freeway for an hour, my longest stretch ever, long enough to get over the jitters. I was surprised to find that I5 was pretty through here with Mt. Shasta catching the setting sun.

Mount Shasta

I pulled into McCloud at a little after 7:00, tallying 10 hours and 311 miles in the saddle. It turns out that McCloud is a beautiful, tiny, historic town. It was deserted, except for two couples meandering along the street. I felt a twinge of apprehension. Would this be one of those romantic vacation spots populated entirely by couples? I crossed my fingers that my room wouldn't be too romantic.

I dragged my bags upstairs and was relieved to find that my room wasn't romantic. On the contrary, it was super feminine. It felt like being in a grandmother's house, safe and cozy. Phew.

The "Hot & Tot" room in the McCloud River Mercantile Hotel, McCloud, California

With 10 hours in the saddle, the last thing I wanted was to climb back on the bike to find food, but I knew I couldn't skip another meal. After skipping dinner last night, all I had eaten today was a little oatmeal and a couple granola bars and crackers. I was famished. Rather than changing, I left the leathers on and set off on the bike in search of food. Luckily, I found the McCloud River Lodge close by.

I walked in and was immediately greeted by the high energy waitress. "It's so great to see another woman rider!" She went bouncing out the door. "I have to see your bike!" Moving a little slowly after my long day, I drifted outside with her, smiling at her enthusiasm. It turned out that she rode a Ninja 600 and rarely had a chance to hang out with other women riders. We happily gabbed away about bikes as we returned to the restaurant, and I settled into a table in the bar.

I ordered a prodigious amount of food and a soda. As I waited for it to arrive, a lady stopped by my table. She was in her early 50's, with long straight hair. She approached shyly, reached out her hand and said, "Much respect."

"Excuse me?" I wasn't sure what she meant.

"I ride on the back," she explained. "But I have a lot of respect for you on your own bike."

Surprised, I thanked her with a big smile, and she gave me some warnings about the deer on the roads at night. My salad arrived, and soon after, I had another visitor – a lady in her early 40's, joined shortly thereafter by her husband.

"I just wanted to let you know that I am very proud of you," she announced emphatically. "You're traveling on your own bike."

"Uh...wow. Thank you!" This was unexpected.

"Aren't you scared?"

I stopped and thought for a moment. "Well, sure. I was scared when I started. But I'm not scared anymore. People are really nice."

It turned out that her husband rode so we exchanged travel stories for a bit before they continued out the door.

After my entree arrived, a man passing by my table on his way out the door shot me a quick, bright smile and a wave. "Shiny side up!"

In between these visitors, my waitress, Wendey, and I continued to talk bikes. I invited her to ride with me the next day, and she regretfully declined, saying that she was busy. As I wrapped up my dinner, a bluegrass session started on the back porch, and I walked to the back door to listen. A few minutes later, I realized that it probably wasn't the best idea to leave my phone out unattended, but when I got back to the table, I found that not only was my phone still there, it now had a twin. There was a second phone on the table. Huh? Wendey returned, explaining that she had had second thoughts. Maybe it would work to ride tomorrow, and could we exchange phone numbers? Sure!

I was exhausted, and the soaker tub back in my room was calling my name. It was time to head back to the hotel. Leaving the Lodge, I felt encouraged and hopeful. It had been several days since I had had a real conversation with someone face-to-face, and I appreciated being welcomed into the community there. Returning to the room, I enjoyed a bath in the decadent tub and curled up in the very comfy bed. I felt cozy and relaxed and fell asleep quickly.

Around 3:00 am, I awoke feeling panicky and scared. It had been months since I had felt this, a deep permeating fear of eternity. Mike wasn't ever coming home. He had been a submariner with the Navy so we were used to spending time apart. I can handle him not being here today and not being here tomorrow...but nevermore? He is lost forever? I don't know why, but sometimes in the middle of the night I find this aspect of death incredibly, thoroughly frightening.

I sat up and swung my legs off the side of the bed, thinking that I would make some tea in the communal room but then remembered the loud wooden floors and didn't want to disturb the other guests. I sat on the edge of the bed for a few moments, rocking in pain. Then I grabbed my book and lay down, reaching for distraction. Eventually, the fear subsided enough for me to slip back into the comfort of sleep. This was a pivotal day in my trip, with tremendous highs, but the work of grieving was not over.

McCloud, CA

Route: Uh...dunno. I was the follower, not the leader today. Destinations: reservoir, river, lake, Mt. Shasta, McCloud River Mercantile Hotel in McCloud. 72 miles.
Favorite destination of the day: The river below the reservoir

After wrestling with my demons the night before, I slept late this morning and had a lazy, languid start to the day. At 9:00, I texted Wendey to see if she was interested in riding and let her know that I was just heading down to breakfast. This hotel wasn't a true B&B since they didn't make breakfast themselves, but they gave a $20 credit per room to spend at two restaurants on the first floor of the building. I chose the diner on the corner and sat in a booth, charmed by the vintage details of the space. It was such a pleasure to have a real breakfast after a week of hotel breakfast buffets, and I splurged on their special of French toast with berries.

The White Mountain Fountain, McCloud, California

Just as I was digging into my food, I heard the waitress say, "We don't allow Harley chicks in here!" Laughing, Wendey swung into the booth dressed in leathers. Awesome! I was so happy to see her. We ate breakfast and planned the day.

Breakfast at the White Mountain Fountain, McCloud, California

I went next door to book another night at the hotel. It felt like a holiday to have a play day with no route planning and no focus on making it to a goal destination for the night. Plus, I was glad to have some more time to explore the small town. And I was excited to have a companion for the road and to get to know my new friend better.

I quickly changed into my leathers and went down to my bike. There was a man sitting on the veranda beside the bike. We made small talk as I hooked up the tank bag, then he said the fated words: "I guess you've seen the oil leak?" Uh...no. He pointed it out. Yep, oil leak. I felt a passing rush of shame that I hadn't noticed it. Mike would have. I wasn't very good at this road tripping stuff. I let it go and examined the leak further.

The oil leak

In a strange way, I was glad to face a mechanical issue. The goal of this trip was to face my fears, and one of them was exactly this situation. What would I do with a mechanical issue? I didn't want to arrive home and still have this lingering question. I didn't exactly *want* something to go wrong, but I wasn't crushed that it had. Now I got to dig into the real stuff.

Wendey rode up, and I pointed out the leak. We noted that the oil wasn't leaking enough to drip on the ground, and she rubbed some of it between her fingers and reported that it was clean – no grit or metal shavings. She pointed out that we had two options: 1) we could scrap the ride and try to contact a mechanic, or 2) we could wipe it clean then ride and see if and how much it continued to leak.

I certainly didn't want to give up my chance to ride with a local guide. At least now, if I got stuck on the side of the road, I'd have some company to send for help. Figuring that it didn't look catastrophic, I decided to ride. I texted photos of the leak to a friend, asking if it was serious, and we rode off.

We took it mellow in the populated areas, but as soon as we got out of town, it became apparent that she was a better rider than me. The morning sun cast long shadows of the tree limbs across the road, and I found the flickering light-and-dark distracting. We passed by green fields and wound our way up into some hills. Coming around corners, I started to find little piles of rocks that the pale, rocky hillsides had shed onto the road. My speed dropped further. I was glad that I had warned her the night before that I was slow.

We rode around the reservoir, filled with shockingly bright turquoise water. She pulled up at an intersection in the narrow roads and waited for me. "Do you want to go down to the river? There might be a little debris on the road," she asked. Shrugging, I said, "Sure!" I was curious what she meant by "a little debris." I suspected that her definition might be different from mine. Didn't the rocks in the road already count as a little debris?

We started down the one-lane curvy road, and, sure enough, within a couple turns, the road became gravel with a tight downhill curve. I slowly crunched across it, grateful for the gravel experience yesterday. Coming across this section a week ago would have given me a heart attack. A little debris...ha! The road became paved again, though still narrow, and soon we pulled over next to a metal pipe handrail leading down the hill.

Below the reservoir, McCloud, California

Wendey asked if I wanted to see the river. "Sure," I said with a few reservations. "But I'm not very good at hiking in motorcycle boots. I might not make it all the way down." She reassured me. "You'll be fine. I used to have problems hiking in boots when I first started too." I made it to the riverbank upright the whole way, though I considered scooting on my butt a time or two.

It was beautiful – really stunning - and I was so glad to be there. Wendey took a couple pictures of me, and as I quickly reviewed them, I looked like a stranger in my own eyes. Who was that girl? She looked like someone I would want to know, standing relaxed on an undeveloped riverbank in motorcycle leathers and a bright smile. (This was quite a change from the last year.) I thought of how far I had come, that when I set out on this journey, I could not have suspected that I would end up here, deep in the forest, in a beautiful spot I never would have found on my own, with a new friend.

The river below the reservoir, McCloud, California

We clambered back up the hillside and checked the oil leak. Still leaking, just a bit. Wendey and I decided to head out to the lake. It was only about 20 miles, and it would give me a chance to see more about the rate of the leak while I had back-up along for the ride.

We headed west on Highway 89 and were quickly caught behind a big rig. She passed, and I wanted to join her but just couldn't see far enough ahead. My insecurities returned with a vengeance. All of the riders that I normally rode with (much more experienced than me) would have passed.

I thought of all the people stopping by my table last night and felt like a sham. "Little did they know that I'm not a real rider," I thought. I had to take a step back and remind myself that I had ridden this whole way. What is a "real rider?" I may not have been able to ride like I wished, but I must have been some sort of rider, "real" or not, to get myself to McCloud. I set aside the doubt and resigned myself to following the big rig until I either found a good long passing spot or caught up to Wendey whenever she pulled off. A few minutes later, I saw her on the side of the road, waiting for me. She joined me on Highway 89, and soon we were turning onto the side roads towards the lake.

We arrived at the lake and walked out to the edge to enjoy the view. Everywhere we had gone, she had greeted people by name, and it was no different here. There was couple in a canoe on the lake, and she said hi to them as they paddled by with their dog.

Wendey and I sat on the rocks by the shore and soaked up the sunshine. She shared stories of her life, and I gradually built a vision of what it would be like to live there.

I shared with her the reason behind my trip, explaining Mike's accident. "It was the day after he returned from the last deployment of his career," I said. My lips twisted into something that wasn't quite a smile. The unexpressed follow-on phrase was, "Can you effing believe it?" She heard my silent sentiment loud and clear and shook her head.

Lake McCloud, California

After lunch, we returned to McCloud, and I bid her goodbye with a big hug and a huge thank you for sharing her neat hometown with me.

Back at the hotel, it was time to see if I could get some extra advice on the oil leak so I set up camp in the communal room, where I spent several hours posting in the motorcycle forum and texting in side conversations about the problem. Some of the possible explanations were truly worrisome. Coolant in the oil...and vice versa? Eek. The consensus was that it was oil coming from the water pump weep hole.

My proposed route for the next day was to hit Etna for lunch then cross over to Soames Bar before heading north again. Several people had told me that the road from Etna to Soames Bar was truly remote, passing through the Marble Mountain Wilderness. I didn't want to ride this route on a bike I didn't trust. I'd call a BMW dealership first thing in the morning and get their advice.

McCloud, CA to Ashland, OR

Route: 120 miles: 89 east (McCloud Falls), 89 west (Mt. Shasta), I5 north, Ditch Creek Road, I5 north, Colestin Rd, I5 north, La Quinta Inn in Ashland

Favorite road of the day: Hmm...not sure there was a favorite, but Colestin was definitely the most interesting road of the day.

I woke early, refreshed from my relaxing time in McCloud. I headed down for breakfast at 7:30 and poked around to find the second restaurant inside the building. I'm so glad I did. It was a combination organic cafe, bookstore, and candy shop. Talk about my dream spot! I ordered an Americano and a breakfast burrito. It was scrumptious: eggs, grilled veggies, goat cheese, and homemade pesto in a grilled tortilla. Sigh of contentment. As I ate, I spread out my maps and considered possible routes.

The organic cafe/bookstore/chocolate shop, McCloud, California

I was really stuck on which way to go. It had dawned wet and looked like more rain to come so my dream route through the Marble Mountain Wilderness was out. Also, I was going to get a late start since I needed to call the dealership when they opened at 9:00. Depending on the outcome of that call, I'd either find a way to get my bike to the dealership in Medford, or I'd have most of the day free to ride. Time would tell.

An ominous morning in McCloud

At 9:00, I called Hansen's, the BMW dealership in Medford. Despite the fact that the place was hopping, they looked at the online photos as we spoke. They were friendly and professional and reassured me that the bike should be fine to get me home. An internal seal was failing in the water pump, but there was no need for an emergency visit to a service department. Phew. This was great news. I was back on the road.

But which road? Still undecided on a route, I decided to gas up and put some air in the tires. As I fiddled with my tires, a bright yellow VW bug pulled up. The guy behind the wheel shot me a smile and said, "So...you know Wendey?" This was a funny side-effect of spending time with her. Since our outing, at least three people had asked how I knew her. I had crossed from the category of "tourist" to "guest of a local".

The guy with the VW asked where we had ridden yesterday. I listed the river and the lake, and he exclaimed that I couldn't leave town without seeing the waterfalls. They were only six miles up the road, and there were lower, middle, and upper falls.

He asked where I was planning to ride for the day, and I explained that I was thinking about visiting the Buddhist temple near Ashland, which Wendey had recommended as a spot to get good photos. "Oh yeah," he said. "It's definitely worth seeing!" Well, I guess I had my route for the day. The falls then the Buddhist temple on the way to Ashland.

I set off towards the falls and found them without any difficulty. He was right; I was glad to have seen them. Very pretty.

Lower McCloud Falls, McCloud, California

It was sunny as I climbed back on the bike, but I could see rain clouds all around, and the radar app wasn't encouraging. I set off hoping to avoid wearing my rain gear...but no luck. The first few drops fell soon after I left so I stopped on the side of the road and broke out the rain gear before I5.

My previous experience on I5 may have made me a little overconfident. This was not a fun ride. It was gusty and started raining lightly. Unpleasant but not untenable. Suddenly, I looked up and saw a wall of dark rainclouds that extended to the ground. I rode into it, gritting my teeth. Pelted by rain and blown around the road, I quickly decided to get off the highway. The next exit had signs for a small airport but no services. I wished that there was a nice, cozy cafe I could hole up in and thought longingly of the cafe back in McCloud. But even if I just ended up standing on the side of the road, I knew I had to get off the highway. It didn't feel safe.

I pulled off, and luckily there was a rest stop with covered picnic tables. Score! I parked and headed for the shelter. It was gusting so badly that it was raining all the way into the far inside corner of the shelter so I left my helmet on. Perversely, I was rather enjoying myself. Isn't this what real road warriors do? Pull off at rest stops during storms? Maybe this meant that I was a real road warrior now! I laughed at the thought. Little ol' me, a road warrior, yeah right!

Inside my rest stop shelter somewhere north of McCloud on I5

About 15 minutes later, the rain lightened. I waited a little while longer, hoping that some of the water on the road would dry, then hopped on the bike to continue.

At exit 796, I left the highway. The GPS directed me through paved, two-lane country roads that ran along fenced fields. I crossed a set of train tracks and soon found the dreaded sign: "Pavement ends."

Well, that answered that question. There was no hope of more pavement down the road. Continue or not? I considered the road. It was well graded gravel, flat and plenty wide enough for two vehicles. I checked the GPS: 2.7 miles to the destination. I really wanted to see the temple so I shrugged and said, "It's only a couple miles." Ha! I was so nonchalant. What a difference this trip has made. MILES of gravel! Of course, it was more than "a couple", closer to three miles, and then there was the return to consider. I held out hope that there might be a different, paved route for returning to the freeway, but I knew that I might be signing myself up for roughly six miles of gravel.

I rolled along the gravel road. It gradually rose. I passed a "narrow" sign and considered turning around, but no, I was doing fine so far. Continuing on, the road narrowed and climbed. I passed a sign that said "slow". I glanced down at the GPS and laughed to find myself doing 7.2 mph. Maybe I should speed it up a bit. I gave it a bit more throttle and rolled along at a blistering 11 mph before my speed crept back down to 7-8 mph. That was where I was comfortable. I looked up and saw the road take an uphill sharp turn beside a sign that said "winding road". Huh, perhaps this wasn't the best idea. The road was now gravel, narrow, winding, and climbing. I promised myself that I'd turn around if it looked like something I couldn't handle, but it still seemed to be okay so far.

The miles counted down on the GPS until the GPS lady said, "You have reached your destination." I thought I saw some prayer flags fluttering on the mailboxes up ahead, but as I arrived at the mailboxes, I saw that they were just red, white and blue ribbons. The side road was marked private, and there was a large NO MONUMENT sign. I had seen those signs occasionally throughout Oregon. I still didn't know what they meant, but I assumed that this one translated as, "Don't bother us, you pesky Buddhists".

I smiled at the situation, cried uncle, and carefully turned around. Even if I could find the temple, it was already after 4:00, and I didn't know how late they accepted visitors. Plus, I saw a weather front in the distance that looked worrisome. I acknowledged that I'm willing to venture into the unknown, but there comes a time when the individual decisions to press on could become bad decisions. It was time to let this one go and head back to the freeway.

The end of the road, for me, at least. (The road flattened out right before I reached this point.) Near Hilt, California

On the way back, I stopped at the railroad tracks to snap some photos. Though I didn't find my goal, it was still beautiful out here.

I merged back onto I5 and quickly climbed into the mountains then down the sweeping switchbacks into Ashland. Pulling into the La Quinta, I saw that I had just beaten the menacing cloud front.

The cloud front I dodged. La Quinta Inn, Ashland, Oregon.

My post on Facebook that evening: "Well, they can't all be amazing days of riding, but today was still an adventure! Battled wind and rain on I5 and rode six miles of gravel, all to visit a Buddhist monastery that I never found." They say it's the journey, not the destination, and that was definitely true today.

Postscript

I later figured out that I had been on the correct road after all. I just needed to continue another two miles to find the Buddhist temple.

Ashland, OR to Tillamook, OR

Route: 347 miles: I5 north, 42 west, 101 north, Ashley Inn in Tillamook

Favorite roads of the day: Highways 42 and 101 (basically, anything other than I5)

In the morning, the TV weatherman gave me bad news. He forecast two days of good weather then three back-to-back storm fronts, bringing a week of rain. This is what I was afraid of with the weather turning.

It was time to book it home. To be honest, I wasn't ready to go home yet. If the forecast had been different, I wouldn't have chosen to return. I reminded myself to live in the moment; today I was still on the road. I was determined to enjoy it.

It was a bright, sunny, crisp morning as I strapped my bags on the bike. I threw my sunglasses on and was happy to hit the road. By now, the bike's seat felt like home, my safe space in the world. This was definitely a change from the past. When I first started riding, simply throwing a leg over made me break out in a cold sweat.

I finally reached the coast, and it was just beautiful. In the sunshine, the views were a real treat. I was torn between the desire to take lots of photos and my goal of getting lots of miles in. When I saw the Sea Lion Caves, it seemed the perfect opportunity to take a break and some photos at the same time. The fresh sea breeze whipped my hair about as I enjoyed the shimmering water, the cliffs, and the distant lighthouse.

The Oregon coast

Sea Lion Caves, Florence, Oregon

Outside the Sea Lion Caves gift shop, Florence, Oregon

Inside the Sea Lion Caves gift shop, Florence, Oregon

After snapping some photos, I took a quick walk through the gift shop. In the corner was a display of homemade signs with painted sayings. One read, "Kiss me good morning and kiss me goodnight." "That's cute," I thought and took a step to move on. Suddenly, I stopped short with my breath caught in my throat, snatched away by a memory. I had totally forgotten that Mike used to come back to bed and kiss me goodbye every day before work. And I would do the same for him if I left first. I stood in the aisle of the gift shop trying to catch my breath. How could I have forgotten this?

It is such a mixed blessing to forget. I hate forgetting any little thing about him, about us. It scares me. It feels disloyal. But yet, if I grasp too hard at holding the memories, the past, I will never move on.

My grief class talked about integrating our losses into our new, meaningful lives. I loved this concept because it meant that I didn't have to leave him behind. I could bring him forward with me. And I have. I carry with me everything that I learned from his life and from his death. How could I not? Still, I struggle with moving forward. How do I navigate creating a new life while still honoring him? It is not easy or simple. Like every step of this grieving process, all I can do is take one step in the direction that feels true to my heart...then take another step...and so on. There is no pre-set recipe for creating a new life after death.

Reaching for my equilibrium, I browsed the rest of the store and bought a package of cocktail-flavored Jelly Bellies as a treat. It was time to keep moving, and the sun and sea air did wonders to freshen my mind and mood.

It was amazing how quickly the miles flowed by when the roads weren't too twisty. For once, I was making better time than I expected. I was in a good groove. As twilight fell on the beautiful day, I pulled into Tillamook and found my hotel. The front desk clerk gave me her last homemade cookie and showed me where to park, between the picture windows and the support columns in front of the hotel. I asked for dinner recommendations, and she suggested Kendra's Kitchen, about a mile down the road. Remembering my experience walking in Willits, I asked if it was safe to walk alone at night, and she reassured me. "We're just a small town here," she said. And I did feel safe.

I quickly changed into street clothes and started to walk. Mountains were silhouetted against the sky to the left and right, and the bright moon was approaching fullness. This was a true marker of how long I had been on the road. I remembered the crescent moon above the mountains when I crossed the Hood River bridge my first night of the trip. And here, on my last night, it was almost full. I soaked in the beauty of the night.

Over dinner, I texted my friend, Buz, and invited him to

come ride with me the next day. We had talked about this possibility before I left, that he might join me for the ride home when I returned. He was available so we decided that I'd travel north on 101; he'd travel south on 101; and we'd try to find each other around South Bend. It was a plan.

After dinner, I walked back to the hotel, savoring the beautiful night, my last of the trip.

Tillamook, OR to Bremerton, WA

Route: 297 miles: 101 north, Miami Foley Road, 53 north (Necanicum), 26 west, 101 north, Astoria bridge, 101 north, 107 east (Montesano), 8 east (McCleary), 101 north (Shelton), 3 north (Bremerton), home
Favorite roads of the day: Miami Foley Road, Hwy 53

The morning dawned bright and sunny. I should have been excited to hit the road, but I found myself dawdling. I knew that I was going home today, and I was just fighting it. My body was pointed towards home, but my heart was pulling me a different direction, back towards the open road. Still, I tried to keep a positive outlook. I had traveled most of today's roads before and knew that they'd be a treat in the sunshine.

From my parking spot, the only way out was the sidewalk. Woohoo! I was irrationally excited for my first ride on a sidewalk, and this silliness started to turn my mood around. As I rolled out and turned onto 101, I was happy to be on my bike. It wasn't a chore to ride. Before the trip, I had reassured myself that if I didn't like it, I could go home anytime I wanted. I told my friends that maybe I'd only spend a night or two away. But

10 days in, I had caught the moto tripping bug in a big way.

My first time riding on the sidewalk. Ashley Inn, Tillamook, Oregon

I finally figured out how to take a self-portrait on the bike.

It didn't take long on 101 to make my way to Miami Foley Road. This two-lane country road twisted through narrow valleys. Much of it was in deep shade, but the morning sunlight cut through to brighten some sections. There must have been water nearby since the air was cool and damp.

I reached Highway 53 and turned right. This was one of Mike's favorite roads, and for the first time on the trip, I pictured him riding with me. Actually, in my mind's eye, we were on the bike together. He must have felt such joy on that road, his soul singing as the bike danced through the corners, throttle and brakes *smooooooth*, body engaged, mind focused, eyes bright, and a grin on his face. I could picture him riding with his friends there, the bikes like playful lightning bugs chasing each other. He felt so close to me.

Finally, I couldn't take it anymore and had to let it out. A few miles from the end of the highway, I pulled over, turned off the bike, and sobbed into my helmet. "God I miss you," I whispered to him. I took off my helmet and dismounted. Taking deep breaths, I walked the clearing. My eyes followed the tall trees up to their tips, where the sun was just peeking through. I drank some water, ate a few Jelly Bellies, took some photos, and then I climbed back on the bike. Nothing to do but move forward, right? That's the only choice.

The sun peeking through the trees, Highway 53, Oregon

The road behind...

And the road ahead

In Astoria, I accidentally turned onto the bridge entrance before I planned to. This is a very high bridge, 196 feet at high tide. All I know is it makes my toes curl in fear! As I started to climb the bridge, I was silently exhorting the traffic before me to keep moving. Unfortunately, we quickly came to a dead stop due to construction. Breathing deeply, I focused on the cars and bridge deck before me, while taking darting glances at the view. Luckily, they didn't keep us long. I have a love/hate relationship with this bridge. The view really is stunning, but I simply don't like heights.

After crossing into Washington, Astoria Bridge in the background

As I traveled north, north, north, I kept a sharp eye out for Buz's HID light and brightly striped helmet. I cruised into South Bend and was thinking of pulling over to wait when I spotted him. Perfect timing! We pulled over next to the "South Bend – Oyster Capital of the World" sign, and I gave him a monster hug. "I made it!" I exclaimed. It felt like an accomplishment – back in my home state riding with a friend. The foreign, challenging part of the trip was over, and I had survived it.

Meeting up with my friend in South Bend, Washington

After taking a few photos, we rolled up the street and parked for lunch. In the parking lot, Buz took a walk around my bike. We talked about the oil leak, and he pointed out that I was going to need new tires soon. Cool! I know this is something that most riders do not celebrate, but it was the first time in my riding career that I had worn through an entire set of tires on my own. These tires had been Mike's. I had found them in the basement after the accident, still wrapped in plastic. In the late spring, as it looked like I was going to work up the courage to start riding the BMW finally, Mike's tires were mounted. (I had purchased the BMW before I was ready for it and rode my CBR250R to work on my skills until I was ready to switch over.)

These tires had kept me safe for almost 4,000 miles this summer, through his memorial trip and now my solo ride. I felt a lot of affection for these tires and, in many cases, trusted them and my bike more than I trusted my own riding skills. I knew that they could handle greater lean angle and speeds than I would be comfortable with. It was nice to know that if I got into trouble, I could "lean and believe" or "when in doubt, throttle out," and the bike would take it in stride.

After lunch, we hit the road and headed up 101 and across 107 to Montesano. As I rode, I could feel the pressure gathering in my chest. We stopped for gas and a restroom break. When Buz walked out of the store, he found me leaning on the ice machine outside, tears slowly trailing from beneath my sunglasses. "I just miss Mike," I told him. "It's okay to miss him," Buz reassured me. "I miss him too." I wiped my face and blew my nose. He asked if I wanted to cut our ride short and just head home, but I said no. It was a beautiful day. And besides, I was in no hurry to get home.

We spent a few hours on the back roads, where my doubts assailed me again. I felt that I was riding terribly. I had spent so much time riding two-up with Mike. I knew how the rhythms of a ride should be, how a bike should feel in the corners. In my mind, there was no doubt that Mike was the definition of a "real rider," and it just wasn't me. No matter how I tried, I couldn't ride like that. At least not now. Give me another 90,000 miles under my belt (like he had), and maybe I'll be there. And maybe I won't. Maybe I don't have the talent; maybe I don't have the temperament (risk tolerance) to ever ride like he did. I won't know unless I continue.

Beautiful fields, Montesano, Washington

Finally, we headed towards home. I knew that this should be my triumphant return, but really...my heart just hurt. It was a physical ache in my chest, tender and sore and without surcease. I was riding towards a home that was empty of him. I missed him terribly. I thought about the trip I just taken and longed to hear him say that he was proud of me. I rode the miles home with tears seeping down my face, soaking into my helmet pads.

As I pulled into my driveway, I knew that I should have been proud of myself for what I accomplished, and tomorrow I would be, but today...I was just sad. I rolled the bike into the garage, snapped a few photos, and pulled my bags off the bike. Then I climbed the stairs and stepped out onto the deck to admire the gorgeous sunset. I had made it home.

Safe and sound in my driveway

Conclusion

To put it baldly, I set off on this trip looking for a reason to continue the fight, a reason to live. I wasn't ready to give up, but there's only so long that you can survive on a diet of blind faith that time will heal. I wanted to know if I had the capacity for joy. I wanted to know if there was beauty in the world. I wanted to know if I could find any forward momentum, any curiosity for the future. I found all of this and more. On those high, remote mountain roads, with the sun warming my back and the pavement unfurling before me...I found joy and beauty and a desire to see what was around the next bend.

I never expected that this trip would put an end to the grief. If only it worked like that – one grand gesture to put it to rest. Grief is a strange and twisty journey. You can't skip any steps to fast forward to the end, if there is such a thing as an "end" at all.

What I hoped for, in my fragile heart, was that I would return knowing that joy was possible. When it feels like life has been nothing but gray for the past, present and foreseeable future, having a dot of color is precious beyond words. I didn't need a full color landscape. I needed to know that color was possible.

That is what this trip gave me...the promise of color. The promise of a life worth living. For now, that is enough. And I am grateful beyond all measure to have it.

A few days after returning, I went to a yacht party with a couple girlfriends. There were DJ's and dancing, and the weather miraculously cleared for a beautiful sail. I enjoyed the music and danced away, both with my friends and alone. As I took a break at the railing, a man approached me. "I love the energy that you're putting off on the dance floor," he said. "You know who you are and what you want." I looked at him quizzically. He could tell all that from my dance moves? But as I thought about it, I realized that yes, people can read the energy you put out, sometimes better than you can yourself. I'm still figuring out who I am, this new person after the accident. But I am comfortable with myself. I am comfortable in my own skin. That is part of what this trip gave me.

Later, another man stopped to talk to me. "This isn't your scene, is it? If you could be anywhere in the world right now, where would you be?" I looked out over the blue water and green hills and told him, "I just returned from a motorcycle trip. If I could be anywhere right now, I'd still be out there, on my bike, in the wilderness."

The precious memories of sunny, solitary moments of joy will accompany me on the journey forward. I have tucked them away in my heart, in reserve for a dark day, when I am low and need a reason to persevere. I carry with me the promise of joy. I carry with me...hope and the seeds of peace.

Postscript

The day after returning, I sat down at my computer and started writing the introduction and first day of the ride report. I wrestled with how honest to be. Finally, I decided to just write what was in my heart and figured that I could delete sections later. But after it was written, I found that I didn't want to delete anything. This was the truth of my experience. Still, it took a deep breath (well, a number of them) and a lot of discipline to bolster my courage to press the "post" button.

I posted the ride report both on my home motorcycle forum (PNWRiders) and on ADVrider. I had been so inspired by the ride reports on ADV that I wanted to give back to that community too. After pressing the "post" button, I sat back and waited to see how it would be received. The comments would determine how honest I'd be in the rest of the report.

The responses were amazing: touching and heartwarming. This encouraged me to continue posting with honesty. As I wrote up each day of the trip, I found myself surprised again and again. I hadn't realized what I had learned from each experience until writing it. There were connections that weren't clear until I relived them from the outside.

In my mind, this post-trip processing was part of the treasure of this trip. I received one set of gifts living the experience, another writing it up, a third through posting it (putting myself out there), and a fourth through your replies and readership. Grief can be a lonely journey. Our society doesn't deal well with death so much of the time I censor myself. "Uncensoring myself" and still being accepted...well, I can't tell you what that means.

Since returning, I have felt better than at any point since the accident. I walked to work on Tuesday morning through the warm rain and felt open and perhaps even hopeful. There has been movement in several areas where I felt stuck before. For one, I have started cooking again – nothing fancy but even making basic food is an improvement. Another is that I am ready to redecorate my bedroom. While the bedroom in McCloud wasn't my style, the comfort and safety I felt there is something that I want to recreate at home. The giant FSU Seminoles head rug at the side of my bed will move on, but the Seminoles stained glass lamp is staying. These are small changes, but small changes are how big changes start. As CS Lewis wrote in *A Grief Observed*:

> *There was no sudden, striking, and emotional transition. Like the warming of a room or the coming of daylight. When you first notice them they have already been going on for some time.*

I hope that this report gave you something - curiosity about a road, inspiration to try a trip of your own, insight into one person's grief journey, courage to step into your own fears, fortitude to fight your demons another day. Whatever you have taken away, I can say that I have gained an equal measure of curiosity, inspiration, insight, courage, and fortitude through the writing. Thank you, dear reader, for joining me.

Part Three:
Reaching for Life

October, 2013 – March, 2014

CHAPTER 53

Energy (!)

October 21, 2013

This week I am BURSTING with energy. I look around in bewilderment. Where the hell did *this* come from? Since the accident, it's been all I could do to muster the energy to peel myself off the couch to go to work or to bed. Some days, it felt like an effort to simply keep my head upright. I probably have more energy in my body this instant than the last year altogether.

I'm so full of energy now...I'm practically vibrating. My fingertips are atingle. I want to exercise, not to energize myself and to unstick myself from the everyday monotony, but to bleed off some of this energy. Saturday in particular I woke feeling GREAT. It's all I can do not to fill this blog post with exclamation points. (!!!) This is the best I have felt since the accident, by FAR.

Why? I don't trust it. Two weeks ago I was struggling with the regular anxiety. Two months ago I was at one of my lowest points. What is different today than then? This journey is so cyclical. I know another low is coming so I don't trust the high. But I want to...I want to be able to relax into the good moments.

Is it sad that I trust the low moments more? That I am more comfortable with the lows? I hope that someday the highs are as close friends as the lows.

CHAPTER 54

Día de los muertos

November 9, 2013

On Halloween a year ago, a friend posted the poem *Día de los Muertos* by Abelardo B. Delgado on Facebook. I loved it so much, I printed out copies to share with my grief class. I love this idea of making friends with death, not in the sense of suicide, but death personified as a way to connect with your lost loves.

This Halloween, I raced around the house trying to piece together a last-minute costume. I didn't have all the pieces to make any full costume I could think of. Finally, I remembered this poem and smiled. I grabbed my grinning skull t-shirt and piled on jewelry from my dearly departed loved ones. Jade earrings from my grandmother. Tennis bracelets, red pendant necklace, and watch from Mike. The angel's wing necklace from his family.

As I layered on each piece, I gently cradled the memories that came with them: Going through my grandmother's jewelry drawer with her, as she told the stories behind each treasure carefully stored in the egg carton bases. Mike surprising me with the bracelets before he went to Afghanistan and the watch when he returned. His family sending the angel's wing necklace last Christmas, in a box with a handwritten inscription: "For when you need extra love - the open heart sends love from Mike + all of us."

This was my own personal take on Día de los muertos. And as I went through the day, I felt draped in love.

CHAPTER 55

Happiness and future plans

November 9, 2013

I've sat down to begin this post three times this week. Again and again, I stepped away without putting "pen to paper". The problem is, paradoxically, that I'm doing okay. Actually, I'm doing better than okay. There is a simmering happiness undershadowing my life right now. It's there bubbling away regardless of the irritations or successes of daily life. In fact, the moments of mundane quietness are when the happiness seems to come to the forefront, like when I'm driving. Nothing triggers the happiness. On the contrary, it is the absence of a trigger, the absence of any action distracting me from my own essence, which provides the space for the happiness to come up.

The happiness is part of the energy that burst out last week. My counselor described it as a dam breaking, releasing my energy so that it can flow again. Yes, amen. That is exactly it. I spent last year bottled up so tightly. It's like a dam broke after my solo ride, at first with the wild outpouring of energy described in my earlier post. Now with this smoother flow of energy.

The "stuck-ness" of last year is starting to release its stranglehold. I tried two new exercise classes last week, started wearing new clothing, and have put on five pounds with my renewed appetite. I have made good progress at work and am almost caught up from a one and a half year backlog. Hallelujah.

Yesterday I noticed that I'm actively scanning for my next personal project. Lots of ideas are bubbling. Redecorate the house, learn to draw, take up classical/flamenco guitar again, travel. Two nights ago, I was getting ready for bed when I remembered a thread from the motorcycle forum; in it, a member who lived in Mexico had offered to host forum members. I sat down and wrote to him right then. The next day, he responded. Yes, he is still hosting people. I looked up flights, and it won't take too many miles to fly for free. My logical side says that I should do more research, but the truth is that I've already made my decision.

For my birthday, I'm going to go ride in Mexico. Writing this statement makes my heart feel tight, bright, and sparkly. Nerves and excitement. Excitement? I didn't know that was possible.

I still don't trust that this upward trajectory is going to continue, but I am starting to relax into it. I'm afraid to talk too much about it. I give the happiness sidelong glances and poke it occasionally to see if it's still there. It's like a guest at a party who might disappear if he gets too much attention. We'll just try living alongside one another for a while before I grow to count on him.

CHAPTER 56

Death and humor

November 18, 2013

Here are two concepts that don't seem to go together: death and humor. They are awkward bedmates, but they certainly do coexist. Just because you're going through a horrifying situation doesn't mean that you've lost your sense of humor.

Part one: absurd humor

Laughing at the absurdities helped me make it through. For example, a week after the accident, I went to the library with my mom, walked up to the reference desk and burst into tears. Taking a moment to gather myself, I managed to choke out, "I need some cheerful books, please!" Something about the absurdity of this situation struck my funny bone. A wildly weeping woman asking for cheerful books?

(The librarian looked at me like I was a crazy lady, but after I explained the situation, she matter-of-factly led me through the stacks, pulling an armload of books that didn't contain romance, death, or motorcycles.)

Part two: crazy humor

Shortly after the accident, a friend who had lost her husband to a stroke a few years ago described her first year of grief: "I was crazy. I thought I was normal; I FELT normal. But looking back now, I was crazy." I took these words to heart. I didn't trust myself. Maybe I was crazy too, even if I felt normal.

Proof of my "craziness" came a couple weeks after the accident. I was at a dinner party with about eight friends, some of whom I hadn't seen since the accident. I was animated as I shared a funny anecdote from the prior week:

I was at the mall shopping for the memorial service dress with my mom. At the checkout counter, the sales lady complimented me on my purchase. "This is such a great dress," she told me. "You can wear it to work after the funeral!" I looked at her, tongue-tied. "It was my boyfriend who died," I explained. "I don't think I'll ever wear it again." "Oh!" She looked at me with a bright smile. "Was he in the military?" [Insert awkward moment of silence.] "Yes," I answered, "but that doesn't have anything to do with how he died." "Well, that's good," she said with a smile, patting the counter reassuringly. What the...? I walked away with my mom and said to her, "People keep telling me that they don't want to say the wrong thing, and I tell them that it doesn't matter what they say. I just appreciate them talking to me. But this lady? She managed to find the wrong thing to say!"

I looked around the dinner table after recounting this little story, and some friends were laughing. But my eye was caught by one friend at the far end of the table. Not only was he not laughing, he looked APPALLED. This is when it hit me: my sense of humor was so off that what I found funny was actually appalling. My life after the accident was so extreme, so far out of the norm, that this story was lighthearted by contrast. My sense of humor was definitely not normal.

Part three: humor and embarrassment

There is a lot of social pressure not to laugh during grief. The people near me didn't want to be disrespectful so they didn't laugh around me, and I didn't want to be inappropriate so I kept my jokes to myself. At first, it was embarrassing that I found anything funny. I wondered what was wrong with me. How could I laugh while Mike was dead?

Only with my closest friends could I let the formal facade down and joke around. For example, when I told my best friend that I was organizing a memorial park bench for Mike, she responded with, "That's perfect! Mike always did like your ass, and now he can be close to it." Ha! I laughed for days over this. It was such a relief to share that humor with her.

On my side, when I was ordering the brass plaque for the bench, I was looking at the order form and trying to decide what it should say when all of a sudden, what popped in my head was those t-shirts that parents would bring home after they went on vacation. What I really wanted the plaque to say was "My boyfriend went to heaven, and all I got was this stupid bench." I didn't share this joke with many people because I didn't want to seem ungrateful for the contributions to the bench. I am enormously grateful. It was just a funny feeling of, "Hey look, I traded my boyfriend for a park bench!" Yeah, it's totally inappropriate and embarrassing that I find it funny.

Part four: inappropriate humor

About five months after the accident, I started to laugh at completely inappropriate jokes about death. Again, I'd look at myself from the outside and wonder what was wrong with me.

But being entrenched in the aftermath of death gave me the freedom to laugh at things that most people shouldn't. It felt deliciously subversive. (Well, as subversive as you can be while not laughing publicly.)

For instance, in January I had lunch with a friend who had lost her mom recently. We found that we shared this affinity for inappropriate jokes. We made a pact to share them with each other since we couldn't share them with the world. Window shopping later that day, we guffawed when we found the two cartoon books, *All My Friends Are Dead*, and the sequel, *All My Friends Are Still Dead*.

Part five: thoughts on humor

I am grateful for humor, no matter if it's crazy, absurd, or inappropriate. It helps to lighten the load and soften the journey. While it's awkward, embarrassing, and uncomfortable, I refuse to give it up just to grieve in a socially acceptable manner.

Perhaps I should go ahead and make my jokes publicly so that other grieving people will feel free to make their jokes too... We could put together our own comedy troupe, specializing in silly, stupid, shocking jokes about death. I'd join. Who else is in?

CHAPTER 57

Just a normal night

November 20, 2013

You ever have one of those nights where you're driving towards home, and your fondest, deepest desire is for _____ to be waiting for you at home? For it to be just a normal night, where you'll open the door and walk in to find your loved one cozy on the couch, pleased to have you home?

I don't want a grand homecoming. I just want to open that door and have life be normal. Just a regular, no-big-deal Wednesday night, with my honey on the couch, about ready to turn in for the night, asking me if I'm coming to bed soon.

I feel like I'm living a version of *It's a Wonderful Life*. I accidentally took a wrong turn somewhere. This isn't the life I was supposed to have. If only I could retrace my steps and find that point where it branched. Maybe somewhere there's an alternate reality where I am living my dream life, my dream normal life. If only there was a way to get there from here.

CHAPTER 58

Baby steps

November 24, 2013

I've been taking more care with my appearance lately. Doing my hair more often than not, adding a little mascara and lip color. I've been feeling better about myself. I'm still not sure if I'm attractive or not, but I'm not embarrassed to show my face to the world.

But I still struggle sometimes. On Friday I went to a concert, an all-ages, electronic music show. I had been looking forward to dressing up. I thought that I would turn it up a notch. Maybe I'd show my friends that I could clean up well. I wore a cute little black and white striped dress with boots and added red lips and a little black eyeliner. Before leaving the house, I took one last look in the mirror and thought tentatively, "Okay, this is working out so far." I felt pretty good.

We ate dinner at a nearby restaurant. The place was jumping so we sat at the bar. Gradually, I started to feel a little uncomfortable, a little exposed. People were probably looking. Maybe I looked ridiculous. I joked with my friend, "I feel like I'm dressed like a 13-year-old." Of course, I was more serious than joking.

I excused myself and went to the restroom. This was probably a mistake; the mirror and lighting were not my friends. My reflection looked old and overly painted. My eyes gazed out, looking for approval. I glanced down, and even my legs looked old, peeking out beneath the possibly-too-short skirt. I spared a moment for a sincere wish, spearing through my heart like a shooting pain, for Mike to be there. For his eyes to light up with warmth, acceptance, desire, and love.

Then I took a deep breath, opened the door, and returned to my friends. Baby steps. I'll get there eventually.

CHAPTER 59

The trial holidays

November 28, 2013

A few weeks ago, I found myself doing math in my head in the pre-dawn hours. As I rose from the depths of sleep, I realized that I was calculating the number of holidays I have spent alone recently. Six of the last eight years I have spent without the person I loved. Today is Thanksgiving 2013; this makes seven of nine. Approaching a decade. No wonder I don't like the holidays.

About a month ago, I took a wrong turn while looking for the restrooms in Sears and stumbled on the lit Christmas trees. Ugh. I cringed and tried not to look at them while passing by. I wondered if any adults truly like the holidays or if the entire thing is a falsehood perpetuated to make kids feel good.

A couple of weeks ago, a friend posted on Facebook how excited she was for the holidays. Quickly, several of her friends commented, agreeing with her. Well, I guess that answers that. Some people look forward to this season all year long.

My experience couldn't be more opposite: this is a season of pain. That sounds far more dramatic than it is. In reality, it's just dreary. It's one "happy" occasion after another, all sad reminders. Mike's birthday is in December, and mine is in January. Adding those to the mix gives us a "celebration" every one to three weeks from November (Thanksgiving) through February (Valentine's Day). An endurance race of holidays.

It is a season that belongs to others, that just doesn't seem to apply to me. Last year, I opted out. I couldn't stand to be around others where I would have to put on a happy face. This year, I'm choosing something different. I'm not throwing myself into the holidays, but I am sampling. I have never purchased my own Christmas tree or my own menorah. I got a menorah in memory of my grandmother and lit it last night, my first time since I was a little girl. I'll probably buy my own Christmas tree as well and add a few meaningful ornaments. Another sign that I'm not avoiding the holidays is that I posted a holiday costume contest with our December bike night. Possibly this is another way to add some cheer to my holiday outlook. We'll see. This is all just a trial.

All I know is that at some point, I have to choose to make a change. The holidays are not going to go away. Either I will spend three months a year in pain, dreading the next happy occasion, or I will find another option. This year, I consider these my trial holidays.

CHAPTER 60

Thanks-giving

November 28, 2013

Today, on Thanksgiving, I am surrounded by an incessant drumbeat of gratitude and thankfulness. My Facebook news-feed has been full of gratitude posts all month, but the crescendo peaked today. The motorcycle forum has multiple thankfulness threads. NBC had a twitter hashtag on the screen all morning for viewers to tweet what they are thankful for. All of their interviews included that question.

It feels like the world has turned into a gratitude bully. YES, I am grateful. I am grateful to a deeply personal extent that surpasses daily Facebook posts. I am grateful in months other than November. But of all days, today is one where gratitude is hard.

Yes, I am grateful. But today, I am also sad.

CHAPTER 61

Mexico, for real

December 2, 2013

When I looked up flights to Mexico a couple weeks ago, my first thought was, "I'll check with Mike then book the tickets." Then I was struck dumb when I realized there's no one to check with. I don't need to coordinate schedules with...anyone. "It can't be this easy...can it?" A bit of a sense of emptiness there.

Tonight, I sat in front of my computer, paralyzed with freedom. I simply couldn't commit to dates without his blessing. I picked up my phone and tried to figure out who I could call to ask this strange question. "Um yeah, could you tell me that it's okay to book these tickets?" As I looked at my phone, it rang with my brother calling. Relief. Perfect. At a lull in the conversation, I explained the situation, fighting tears, repeating, "I know it's stupid," and "I know it makes no sense." But simply talking it out helped me get past the block.

I just booked my tickets. Pressing the "purchase" button, I felt a sense of preternatural calm. But looking at the confirmation page....

Holy shit, I'm going to Mexico to ride a motorcycle. I'm

about to jump out of my skin with nerves and excitement. (!!!)

This strange and twisty journey is taking me to destinations I never imagined.

CHAPTER 62

The light in your eyes

December 6, 2013

A couple of nights ago, I grabbed a beer with a friend. We caught up on the latest in her love life, and she mentioned how much she enjoyed visiting her beau at his band practice. "He lights up," she described. Instantly, I clicked into what she meant. "That's how Mike was about riding," I told her. "That's why I never would have asked him to quit. Why would I want to steal the light from somebody's life? Just for the sake of safety? Safety is a myth. There are no guarantees."

Of course, there's no need to be reckless. When we rode together, it was always in full gear, on a well maintained bike, with the suspension properly set for our combined weight. We took all the precautions we could before riding, then we mounted the bike, set aside the worry, and reached for joy. Some would say that riding at all is reckless. Some would say our speed was reckless. I say that we were content with our joint risks. We had no regrets.

A number of months ago, someone posted a thread on the motorcycle forum asking if he should quit riding after becoming a parent. The responses were heartfelt and honest. People shared their stories of riding with their parents and how it brought them closer, stories of how they stopped riding while their own children were young. Here is my response:

> *I can't speak to this question as a parent, but as a partner of someone who lost their life riding, I can offer my perspective. I think much of it depends on what riding means to you and what it does for you.*
>
> *If riding turns your life from mundane black and gray to Technicolor, if it makes you a better person/partner/father with less pent-up frustration from the day, if you would have regrets and resentment for leaving riding...then it would not be a gift to your family to give it up.*
>
> *In my case, I can honestly say that, even knowing how our story ended, I would not have asked him to quit riding. There are other "what ifs" that play out in my mind, but this isn't one of them.*

This morning, the quote of the day drove home this point:

"A ship in port is safe; but that is not what ships are built for."

-Grace Hopper, US Navy Rear Admiral (1906-1992)

Mike loved riding, with a fierce, passionate joy. Sitting at home "safe", with the light extinguished from his spirit...that is not what Mike was built for.

CHAPTER 63

Videos

December 11, 2013

Last night, I found the five videos Mike shot with his Go Pro camera mounted to his helmet. Three of them were of me on my very first ride on the BMW, and two were of a group ride out to Neah Bay. Also, yesterday morning, I finally watched a friend's video of Mike and me riding two-up.

Watching the two-up video, it felt like watching a slow motion video of a hummingbird, something so beautiful out in the wild. We were smooth and graceful and free. Our riding was everything that I remembered and more. I watched that video and thought, "I was fearless."

Watching the videos that he shot... He was in the lead for the group ride so the video shows his hands on the grips and the road ahead. I had forgotten how under control the bike felt in his hands. It was a sense of relief to watch it, that everything was right with the world. "This is how riding is supposed to be," I thought.

Watching the video of myself... I saw how far I've come. I remember that first ride on the BMW. I was so scared that I

rode the entire first section with my hips askew on the seat because I was afraid to shift my butt while moving. At the end of
the ride, I dropped the bike in the gravel alleyway outside our
driveway. I was stopped, and my foot slipped on the gravel so
it was a slow motion tip-over. It was a different perspective to
see it all from his viewpoint. After I dropped the bike, he came
and picked it up and steadied it so that I could dismount, then
he picked up the broken indicator cover.

This video was a tease. I longed to see HIM, but I could see
his boots and legs and hands, and the audio picked up a few
words. It was still precious. It was him alive and whole and complete, full of everything that made him himself. In the moment
he was videotaping, it would have been nothing to reach out
and touch him. It would have been just a moment's impulse.
How I long for that now, just to reach through the screen, turn
the camera on him, and tell him to never turn it off. Just to reach
through the screen and gather him in my arms.

CHAPTER 64

I hate it when...

December 11, 2013

This post is pure venting. I drafted it in reaction to a thread on the motorcycle forum entitled "I hate it when." Forum members use it to vent about silly things that irritate them - like people who wait until the last second to merge. I find the thread entertaining, but it also gives me this almost irresistible urge to post what REALLY bothers me - not the funny, universal irritations but the real deal.

If I were to post the truth, here's what my list would look like: I hate it when...

...the holidays roll around. This includes birthdays and every other date that is supposed to be happy.

...everyone in a conference leaves en masse to call their significant others.

...couples complain about being apart. Chances are extremely good that they have more communication than Mike and I had when he was on the submarine. (The worst stretch was several months of one email per month.) So... they don't have much to complain about, even aside from the fact that long distance is better than dead.

...couples complain about saying goodbye. They will have a homecoming. Do you know what I would give to say goodbye just one more time, knowing that he would be coming home again?

...couples complain about being together, about each other. Life's too short. Be with someone who makes you happy. If they make you happy, don't sweat the small stuff.

I hate...the fact that it's STILL so damn hard. The fact that one split second of miscalculation brought years of pain – and not just to me.

CHAPTER 65

Birthday Number Two

December 16, 2013

Today was Mike's birthday. Birthday number two since he died. He would have been 37 today, but he will always be 35. I did the math in my head in the shower this morning and realized that by now he would have been on shore duty again. We probably would have moved in August. In an odd way, I'm still counting towards his Navy retirement. His retirement date no longer matters, but it will hurt when that day comes. Or at least, it hurts thinking of that day coming. What do I know about how I'll feel in the future? I can barely keep track of today.

Today, I was bracing myself to see a lot of birthday posts on his Facebook wall, but that didn't happen. I think there were a total of 14, including mine. My post was "Happy birthday, baby. I still love and miss you every day." I included a photo of our hands clasped together as we walked on the beach.

It was a quiet day, all told. I had thought that people might reach out to me today. I posted Mike's riding videos in the motorcycle forum. Maybe people would see that I was having a tough time. Two people responded to the thread. My office manager texted me this morning, and my mom checked on me with texts throughout the day. Mike's ex-wife sent me flowers, the most touching moment of the day.

This afternoon, I left work early to visit his memorial bench at the local park. I stood on the shoreline and watched the golden reflections of the sunset flicker on the water. "Where are you, baby?" I asked him. "Are you the water lapping at the shore? Are you the air kissing my cheek?" The motion of the water calmed me. I watched the birds fly low over the water and was surprised by the sound of a sea lion breathing. He broke the surface three times in the distance.

Walking back to my car, I carried my phone and wished that it would ring with someone checking on me. I just wanted someone to call or invite me over. I just wanted some connection to combat the horrible loneliness. But maybe it's too late for that. Maybe by birthday two, I'm supposed to be doing better. But it did feel lonely. And empty.

CHAPTER 66

"Why We Ride"

January 8, 2014

Last weekend, we showed the movie, *Why We Ride* at our bike night. I was excited to see it. It is a documentary about riding, spanning a variety of riding styles, from racing to touring two-up and riding with families. The movie was touching.

One man in the film described an early date with his future wife. They were riding two-up and had stopped at a farm stand to buy some fresh cherries. She fed them to him one-by-one as they rode. "It was one of the most romantic times of my life," he said.

The movie went on to show families camping and riding dirt bikes together. It closed with an older man describing riding with his daughter. He said that he had given her her first ride and hoped that when she grew up, she'd give him his last ride.

The credits started to roll, and I leaned forward in the dark room and cried, forehead braced on my knuckles. The lights came up, and I tried to get control of myself before anyone noticed. Suddenly, a body dropped into the seat beside me, and an arm came around my shoulders and pulled me in. I relaxed into the shoulder and sobbed.

I can't tell you what this meant. It's been over a year since I have cried in someone's arms. People have tried to hug me when I cry, but I haven't been open to it. I sit stock still, and they awkwardly drape themselves over me, like a flag over a tree that won't bend with the wind. I don't know why I haven't been able to accept what I desperately want.

But that hug after the movie...I can't tell you how precious it was. I have replayed it in my mind's eye, wringing all the comfort possible from it. Though embarrassing to cry in front of a room of riders, it was worth it for that hug...to not carry the pain alone, even for only a few moments.

CHAPTER 67

Confession time: holidays in review

January 10, 2014

I have to be honest about the holidays before I can move forward. While I was doing well for a couple months, the holiday season could not have affected me more profoundly. I had thought that with the highs getting higher, the lows wouldn't be so low, but that wasn't the case. I found myself on a downward slide over a period of weeks, culminating with night after night of crying on the couch and thoughts of suicide. It scares me that I reached that point again.

The kick-off of the holidays, with their intense focus on family, coincided with my social calendar being a ghost town. I either spent the weekends home alone or working. It didn't help that my gift for Mike's family was thumb drives of photos of him. Of course, this meant that I had to go through the photos - on my new computer, old computer, new phone, old phone, and Mike's computer. Ultimately, I was able to assemble the photos and send them off in time for Christmas. But this was pretty much all that I accomplished, other than sending Christmas cards. I purchased no other gifts in December.

I backslid into bad habits: stayed up too late and had difficulty focusing at work. Fits of weeping swept over me at random times. The most awkward one happened at the dentist's office, WHILE the hygienist was working on me! It's funny to think of it now, though it was embarrassing at the time. I just had to have patience with myself.

My social life started to pick up again the week before Christmas, and Christmas itself was fine. Nothing special but not terrible – so I'll take it. The depression started to lift on Christmas, and I'm on the upswing now.

Lessons learned:

- When I am super low, I don't reach out because I couldn't handle it if the person wasn't available. And when I'm feeling okay, I don't reach out because it feels surreal that I would ever be that low.

- I'm a year and a half into this, and I still haven't figured out *how* to reach out - the actual mechanism for reaching out. I did start an email exchange with someone on the motorcycle forum the week before Christmas, and that helped.

- I'm reading another grief advice book now, and it offers the suggestion to have people on tap that you can call if there are certain times of day that are difficult. This is an excellent idea. Their example was dinner time or bedtime, which can be difficult if you are used to a companion at those times. My difficult time of day is generally about 10:00 pm. This is another reason I have trouble figuring out who I should reach out to. I don't want to wake anyone or disturb their evening. It's not a normal time for the phone to ring.

- Next year, I hope to be doing well enough to entertain. This year, I couldn't have completed the planning, and I simply didn't have the force of will to carry through with the preparations. But I know that it would help a lot if I could host dinners and hold a holiday party.

Looking back, I can see that I was in some sort of crisis. I wasn't sitting on a ledge, but I wasn't well.

And now, in mid-January, I am doing better. My social life is full again. My energy is coming back up, and I smile more easily and simply feel lighter all around. Now, I don't want to share this post because I am not in crisis anymore. The whole episode feels a bit like a fantasy, and it seems silly to share it and possibly worry people. On the other hand, if this blog is supposed to record an honest journey of grief, it is dishonest and unconscionable to hide this. It is part of the journey, just as valid as the highs.

Postscript...

On New Year's Eve, I found myself at the hardware store. I went for a single grommet and left with a grommet...and a basket of Christmas decorations: a tree, wreath, and ornaments. They are the most non-traditional decorations you could imagine - bright and multi-colored, like someone mixed the Day of the Dead with Christmas. I couldn't help myself – the funny little ornaments drew me in. I placed them in the basket with a wavery smile. At home, I didn't unpack them – just tucked them away for next year. Buying these decorations is an act of hope. Despite how low the holidays were, I keep reaching for a way to make them my own, to give them personal meaning, to twist them from a punishment imposed from the outside to a celebration engendered from the inside. There are no guarantees that next year will be better, but I'll keep trying.

New Year's Eve ornament shopping

CHAPTER 68

Overdue, no more

January 15, 2014

Yesterday I finished drafting my last overdue report. It's taken almost one and a half years to catch up on the backlog of work since Mike's accident. What a relief. It doesn't seem real yet.

This is major. For over a year, I've pushed back against taking on anything new. I hunkered down and slogged ahead, focused on treading water on current tasks, while oh-so-slowly catching up on multiple overdue reports. My clients were amazingly patient. I am so grateful. Not a single client complained or left, though I wouldn't have blamed them in the slightest.

Now, I give myself permission to focus on moving forward with current projects and future business development. What a change from one morale-sapping overdue report after another. What a change from starting almost every client email with an apology for the delay. This is a major shift in mindset from focusing on the past to the present and future.

While I welcome this shift, it does not feel natural yet. Rather than bursting forward, today I was flailing about a bit, unsure of how to set my priorities without the drumbeat of overdue dead-lines. This new way of thinking will take practice.

But it is good. It is something to celebrate. It makes me feel hopeful. Maybe I won't want to quit anymore. Maybe I'll enjoy my work again. I have a great job, but the grief sucked the joy out of it, along with the rest of my life. I hope that this new stage will be a breath of fresh air.

CHAPTER 69

A surprise

January 19, 2014

Yesterday was my very first surprise birthday party. A friend had asked if I wanted to go out to dinner for my birthday so we scheduled a meal with our parents. It was a lovely family day, with a boat ride up to the restaurant as a special treat.

We arrived at the restaurant and filed upstairs to our table. When I rounded the corner, a table full of my friends yelled, "SURPRISE!" It was wonderful. I felt very loved, surrounded by family and friends who had all taken time out of their holiday weekend to celebrate with me. There were cards and gifts and a homemade cake bright with candles. My heart was full.

This dinner was the antidote to the loneliness I felt over the holidays. A reminder of the good in my life. I am grateful.

CHAPTER 70

A tropical adventure: my second solo(ish) trip

This is the third and final ride report. As with the others, it was originally posted on the motorcycle forums and has been edited here for brevity.

Drafted February 1, 2014 through February 16, 2014

The Background

For this trip, I flew to Mexico and stayed with some motorcycle forum members I had never met before. My hosts were Lee and Christine, a couple from Oregon who moved to Mexico about 10 years ago. Lee is an avid motorcyclist who has a standing offer for PNWRider forum members to come down, stay with him and his wife, and ride his bikes with him. He owns three sport bikes: GSXR-750, ZX-10, and ZX-14.

I wrote to Lee in November, asking if he was still hosting forum members. He assured me that he was, and we corresponded for a bit. He shared a photo of the house, one of the bikes, and one of their four dogs. After settling on the dates for the trip, I booked my tickets in December for traveling at the end of January.

About a week before departing, Lee emailed to let me know that he had some good news: another motorcycle forum member and his wife, Del and Andrea, would be down at the same time as my visit. Well, cool! We'd have a little PNWRiders Mexico group.

The Preparation

I expected that it would be easy to pack for this trip. After all, how hard could it be to pack for a week in Mexico? Throw some summer clothes in a bag, add sunscreen and motorcycle gear, and done. Easy, right?

Don't ask me how, but I managed to make it a major chore. None of my clothes seemed to work together; I couldn't figure out which gear to bring; and there was no obvious best solution on suitcases (checked, carry-on, backpack, etc.).

This packing indecision went on-and-on. I couldn't figure out what my issue was. I travel often for work and know how to pack. Finally, a few days before I left, I was texting a friend, describing my revolving wheel of indecision. He responded, "Breathe. It's only a week."

Suddenly, I knew what the problem was. In the back of my mind, I was expecting Mike to meet me there, and I wanted to look cute for him. A rush of tears, resolving into deep breaths. Let it go, let it go. I reminded myself that I had no one to impress there, and it was only a week. After this breakthrough, I was able to pack in a couple of hours.

And one final note about the preparations: Since the accident, I've been loath to spend my hoarded miles, but putting them towards this trip felt completely fine. I couldn't figure out why. A week before leaving, I realized that the reason I was okay spending my miles on this trip was that I had been saving them to go to Mexico with Mike after he returned from his last deployment.

Riding bikes in Mexico is my dream, not Mike's, but traveling to Mexico...that's a dream I had with him. I hadn't even realized it, but yet again, I was pursuing the dreams/goals I'd had for us. It wasn't a conscious decision, but since the accident, one-by-one I have been completing those unfinished dreams. Wrapping them up and tenderly putting them away.

This trip was a leap into the unknown. On day one, I boarded that plane with no information about the town (except that friends had traveled there and enjoyed it) or my hosts (except that others on the forum had stayed with them and given positive reviews). Like my first solo ride, I wanted to step into the unknown and see what was waiting for me. Who would I meet? Would I be able to handle the riding? How would my rusty Spanish hold up? Would I be lonely in a strange land?

I flew to Mexico on January 25th and returned January 31st, richer with an amazing cultural experience, greater confidence in my riding, dear new friends, and an admirer among la policía (the police). Yes, dear reader, this is my poor attempt at foreshadowing. Read on to learn more about my adventure.

Day One:

Bremerton, Washington, USA to Barra de Navidad, Jalisco, Mexico

Boarding the plane in Seattle, I wasn't nervous. Now that the preparations were over, I was relaxed and looking forward to seeing what came next. I was traveling towards a complete mystery. I hadn't seen a photo of my hosts, had never met Del, and hadn't seen a photo of the inside of the house. While I was curious, I was content to let the mysteries reveal themselves in their own time. Still, I wondered if I was crazy to do this.

A foggy morning in Seattle, Washington

The view from the airplane window: The landing strip in Manzanillo, Mexico is right by the beach.

Lee and Del came to the airport to pick me up. Lee had explained that he was tall with gray hair and would be in an orange shirt. Sure enough, he was easy to spot. I eagerly took in the views on the drive from the airport to Barra de Navidad.

At the house, Lee showed me my room, where I about passed out from how nice it was. When I was imagining what might be awaiting me, I was crossing my fingers that there would be a bed, though I would have been fine on a couch too. I had NO expectations of anything like this.

I had a beautiful, bright bedroom with a king-sized bed, a huge en suite bathroom, and a walk-in closet. There were two little interior balconies that overlooked one of the living spaces and an exterior balcony with a wonderful view of the backyard, canal, mountain, and resort across the water. I felt guilty that I had the nicest guest bedroom for just me, when Del and Andrea were a couple. They were staying in a smaller bedroom with bath next door.

The view from my room, Barra de Navidad, Mexico

As we relaxed in the backyard, Lee said to me, "I have to come clean with you, Candiya." Now, Lee has a lively sense of humor so I thought another joke was coming, but instead he explained that he had serious degenerative back problems and was scheduled for surgery soon. A week ago, he had been on crutches so in order to make sure I had someone to ride with, he had invited Del down. Oh my! It turned out that Del and Andrea had scheduled their trip around mine. I was overwhelmed by the generosity of all four of them.

The conversation topic of the day tended to center on one motorcycle accident or crazy thing that they had seen on the roads after another. I gradually built a mental list of **Things to Be Careful of When Riding in Mexico**. Note that all of these came with accompanying stories of avoiding them or crashes caused by them.

- Large speedbumps ("topes")
- Potholes
- Rocks/boulders shed off of hillsides
- Sand
- Vegetables (crates of tomatoes falling off trucks)
- Fruit (a truck carrying oranges went off the road and spilled its load)
- Diesel dribbled along the road from containers leaking in the backs of trucks going uphill
- Big animals (cows/horses), small animals
- Trucks or traffic stopped around blind corners
- Cars coming out of side streets without looking
- Cars with left turn blinkers on, which might mean that they're turning left or might mean that they're giving you permission to pass
- Cars/buses cutting the yellow in the corners

Listening to these stories, I became more and more nervous. By the end of the evening, Del offered to take me two-up the next day if I was too nervous to ride. This offer was a serious contender because then I'd be able to see the condition of the roads and how traffic worked in Mexico without also riding a strange bike. (Del is a control rider and motorcycle instructor so I felt comfortable with his skill level for riding as a passenger with him.)

I had come all the way to Mexico to ride motorcycles, and I would be very disappointed in myself if I didn't do it. Plus, Del had come all the way from Portland to ride with me. How embarrassing if I didn't ride. But I also knew from past experience that if I forced myself on the bike when my nerves were overwhelming, it wouldn't go well. Tension makes everything tight and jerky, which motorcycles don't like.

I slept restlessly, waking every two hours, until my alarm went off at 6:15 am. The morning of truth had arrived. Would I ride or not?

Day Two:

Barra de Navidad to Playa Tenacatita

I woke feeling lighter and more positive than the night before, though still nervous. I decided that I'd sit on the bike and feel the controls then decide if I wanted to ride. The fact that this was the shortest planned ride of the week with the least traffic made me feel that if I *was* going to ride, today would be the best time to start.

I climbed on the yellow GSXR and tested out the brake lever – a little more travel than mine. I felt the pull of the clutch – tougher than my bike. I lifted the bike off the stand to feel the weight - not too much heavier than my bike. I could do this. I decided to give it a shot.

We rolled out with Del first on the black ZX-14, then Lee on the green ZX-10, then me. Riding down the side streets, I was SO nervous - don't think I could have been stiffer. When we got to the main road, Lee turned and gave me a thumbs up. "Yes," I nodded. "I'm good." We headed down the main street, and this huge grin came over me. "I'm riding in Mexico!" Even if I didn't ride again this trip, I had met my goal.

We crossed through a few small towns then Lee split off to meet another friend who would be riding with us, and I continued on with Del. The two-lane highway wound up into the mountains, with lush foliage bordering the road. My grin wouldn't stop. The highway reminded me of the roads in the old movie, *Romancing the Stone*.

Eventually we left the highway and headed towards the ocean. Pulling up on the gritty hardpack of the parking area, I climbed off my bike and wanted to jump up and down. Hell yeah, now THIS was riding in Mexico! Playing it cool (not), I asked Del to take a picture of me. I'll be honest; I love this picture. This is when I realized that the goal I had put in motion months ago - to ride in Mexico - had been achieved. Actually, this goal was much more longstanding that that. I've been dreaming of riding in Latin America since I first discovered the ride reports in the ADVrider forum, over three years ago. I just never would have thought I would ever be able to do it. It still doesn't seem real.

Success! Playa Tenacatita, Mexico

After a few more photos of the beach, we started back. Almost immediately, we found Lee and his friend, Gilberto, and shortly thereafter, we pulled over for a soda and a break at the shaded tables of a roadside restaurant.

Our rest stop near Playa Tenacatita, Mexico

Pulling back into the house, I switched off the bike, dismounted, and started jumping up and down. "I did it! Thank you so much, Lee! You helped make a dream come true!" I gave him a big hug.

We had left at 8:00 and were home by 10:30, just about the right length for me. I was hot and starting to melt. My heavy winter textile gear just didn't have enough ventilation.

I cooled off by relaxing in the pool, chatting with Andrea and Del. They have been married 27 years and are obviously still in love, like Lee and Christine. They share that easy and relaxed enjoyment of each other, reliance on each other, and trust and respect of each other that's impossible to miss. Seeing them together made me smile. It's good to see a solid couple. It also reminded me of what Mike and I had. I found myself using my camera as a distraction. It would have been wonderful to be here with him.

The pool

When we headed into town for dinner, Christine and I swung by the one ATM in town, where I was very lucky my ATM card worked. I should have changed some money before traveling. We grabbed a water taxi and crossed the laguna to Restaurante Colamilla. It was beautiful.

Barra de Navidad, Mexico

The pier for the water taxi, Barra de Navidad, Mexico

Returning on the water taxi, with the warm dark air pressing against us as the engine pushed us through the water, I tried not to notice how romantic it was. Or would have been. Snap, snap, with the camera.

The ride home on the water taxi, Barra de Navidad, Mexico

Tomorrow would be a longer ride. I was still nervous but not nearly as much as before. I knew that I could handle the bike, though it was faster than mine. But there would be more heat, more traffic, and the ride would be longer. Still, I was excited to see more sights.

Day Three:

Barra de Navidad to La Huerta and La Manzanilla

I started the day in tears. Well, actually, I started the day feeling pretty good but ended up in tears before getting on the bike.

I was hanging around the breakfast table as Lee was gearing up, when he asked if I knew the story behind the blue model bike in the glass case behind him. I shook my head, and he shared with me that he had lost a son, and the bike held his ashes.

Stunned, I immediately flashed on the urn at Mike's service in Kansas. How I had taken photos of it in the church, even though it was probably completely inappropriate, simply because it would be my only chance. Even though I had sat in the front row of the military service in Bremerton, I hadn't realized that the urn was there. It didn't dawn on me that I'd missed it until the next morning, when it was gone.

I remembered, in the days immediately after the accident, Mike's mom asking what wording they should put on the urn, what Mike would have liked. Just one of the many questions for which I had no adequate answer. We ultimately decided on his full name and rank, with the inscription below, "But to Loved Ones, Mike/Daddy".

Sitting in that church in Kansas, I watched Mike's cousin carry the honor and weight of the urn to the podium, struggling to maintain his countenance. Then I laid eyes on it for the first time and just sat in the wooden pew, my body heavy and unresponsive, as I tried to come to terms with the reality of it. That urn wasn't just *in honor* of him. It *was* him. It still isn't real.

I listened to Lee share the story of his son, and my heart ached for him. He closed by saying, "You have to keep living." Then we headed out to the bikes, where I broke into tears. Poor Del was already outside and had no idea why I was crying so I quickly explained. Christine asked if I was okay to ride, and I nodded. The morning was cool and fresh, and I knew I'd be okay once I got on the road.

The first destination of the day was La Huerta. We rolled through the little towns then up into the twisty hills again. I felt bad for Del, stuck behind me in the twisties. I just couldn't seem to get in a good groove so was going really slowly. Eventually, he passed me, and he and Lee passed a truck. I'm pretty conservative when it comes to passing so it took me a little while to find a good spot. A few turns later, I saw the guys pulled over on the side of the road waiting for me.

As I rolled to a stop, they walked up, one to each side of the bike. With no preamble, they launched into a list of riding tips, shotgun style. It made me smile, and I genuinely tried to take in the advice. I needed to improve and really wanted to feel more comfortable out there.

Soon enough, we arrived in the town of La Huerta. What an experience rolling through the narrow, brick-lined streets, with blue flags strung above for blocks on end. Eventually, we found the town square.

La Huerta, Mexico

We rested and enjoyed a soda then decided to head along to La Manzanilla to visit the crocodiles. Back on the twisty, tropical highway, Lee and Del again passed a truck, and by the time I found a good passing spot, they were long out of sight. It was really relaxing to roll along by myself and gave me a small taste of what it would be like to travel in Mexico alone. I was perfectly content.

Lee and Del were waiting at the turnoff to La Manzanilla. We rolled into town, parked, and checked out the "cocodrilario," I snapped some pictures of the crocodiles through the chain link fence.

Next, Lee wanted to stop by a construction site, where a friend was on the crew building a beach house. Pretty soon the brick road turned into a dirt road. I thought, "I'm riding a dirt road on a borrowed sport bike. Now *that's* trust!" I was as careful as could be and arrived without any problems.

The dirt road to the construction site, La Manzanilla, Mexico

The house under construction faced this beach. La Manzanilla, Mexico

As we were getting ready to leave, I considered asking for help turning the bike around on the dirt but coached myself, "No, Candiya, you can do it." Luckily, the road was smooth at that spot, and I didn't have any problems. I let Lee and Del go first, and before I took off, I glanced up to find that all the workers on that side of the house had conveniently decided to take a break. They were all standing around watching to see if I could actually ride a bike. I told myself, "Don't you drop this thing now, with an audience!" And I headed off with no mishaps. Phew!

This ride was a couple hours longer than yesterday. We left at 8:00 and returned at about 12:00. Back at the house, we quickly changed and headed out to lunch. This lunch was a special treat because Lee and Christine had invited the police to join us. They are good friends with the female police captain, and she brought the other two police officers who were on patrol with her so there were three of them. What a wonderful cultural exchange! I sat next to an officer, A., who spoke little English, so he was patient with my Spanish. Del, Andrea, and I left the meal feeling that this was one of the highlights of our trip.

Back at the house, Del asked if anyone wanted to go canoeing. Andrea had to work so I volunteered. Crossing the lagoon, I began to learn a bit about Del's adventurous side. First, he suggested that we could pull into the little beach and portage across the malecon (esplanade) to ride the waves on the bay side with the surfers. The wind was up so I wasn't too sure about that idea. Well, why don't we go see what's around the end of the malecon? Sure, we can do that. When we got to the end of the malecon, he said, "Let's just go until we see the surfers." So...we started heading that way.

The little waves were breaking over the front of the canoe, and warm seawater filled my lap and my seat. I eyed the sharp rocks lining the malecon with distrust. "I'm not so sure about this," I said. "Hey, look at the buoy," he responded. "Let's just go around the buoy!" So...we started paddling towards the buoy. The wind was getting worse as we left the protection of the rocks, and finally, I laughed and said, "abort, abort!" We were actually pretty close to the buoy, but by then, he was saying things like, "Hey, we should paddle to Melaque sometime!" Now, Melaque is all the way across the bay. I was pretty sure if I didn't put the brakes on, we'd have ended up in Puerto Vallarta, or maybe even San Diego! Instead, we turned back to the protected lagoon, explored some of the canals, and headed back to Lee and Christine's.

Back at the house, we changed for dinner then headed out to do some sightseeing at the Grand Bay resort and golf club. The craftsmanship that went into building the club house at the golf course was truly beautiful.

Sightseeing at the golf course, Barra de Navidad, Mexico

Dinner was at a restaurant called Los Caracoles. Lee had explained that there are lots of cooks in his town but few chefs. This restaurant was led by a gifted chef, and I quickly learned what he meant. The dishes were beautiful and dramatic. I had the catch of the day, which was served with two sauces, a corn sauce and a lobster sauce. It was one of the best fish dishes I've ever had.

Full and sated, we returned to the house, where I did a little work and babied my swollen, bite-ridden feet. What a stupendous day.

Day Four:

Barra de Navidad to Peralu...kinda

The ride today was supposed to be a bit longer - a couple hours each direction. We set off, and I simply wasn't able to make the bike do what I wanted while also being relaxed. I tried to remind myself: "eyes up-up-up!", relaxed arms, stay away from the yellow centerline. It just wasn't coming together, and I imagined my companions being frustrated at my slow pace and lack of improvement/progression despite their excellent tips.

I was following Del when he decided to change tactics. He sat up and started making the hand signals I've seen from control riders on the track. Gesturing to his eyes and pointing where to look, exaggerating his relaxed arms, and so on. It was one of those moments that's absurd and wonderful and magical all at once.

Here I was, riding through a jungle in Mexico with my own control rider. Seriously, who gets to do this?? I felt like the luckiest girl in the world. A moment of intense gratitude passed through me. I had walked into the unknown, had boarded that airplane and stepped into the mystery. And this was waiting on the other side. I could have missed this entire experience and never known it, had my fears held me back.

We continued on until we came up to a truck, which Del passed, no muss - no fuss. I envied Lee and Del their passing skills. Sigh. Recruiting my patience, I waited until I found a passing spot that was comfortable.

Eventually, I came to a long, flat, straight stretch and saw that they had pulled over to wait for me. Lee waved me to keep going so I did. A few seconds later, he passed me. Vrooom! Next, Del was going to pass. I was going about 60, and Del was cruising by me in the other lane, just relaxed and steady, maybe 65. When he was right beside me, I heard a snap-kerchunk, like when a chain derails on a bicycle. He looked down at his foot and coasted to a stop, and I pulled up behind him.

"What's wrong?" I hollered through my helmet.

"I lost my chain," he responded.

"What?" I seriously thought I'd misheard him. Does that actually happen? I looked down at his bike. Sure enough, no chain.

Something's missing here...

By then, Lee had come back to us, and they went walking down the road looking for the chain. They found it and returned carrying the forlorn, droopy-looking thing. In my ignorance, I asked Del if he'd be able to fix it on the side of the road. "No, I don't think so," he answered.

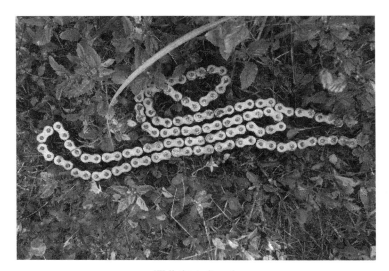

Well, this isn't good...

We were so very lucky, in so many ways. The chain could have caused his back wheel to lock up. The highway behind and ahead of us was full of blind curves with no shoulders. Things could have gone very badly. If this had to happen, this was absolutely the best case scenario and the best location. I was also glad it hadn't happened when Lee was riding alone.

We all talked it over and decided that Lee would go back to get his truck and trailer. I decided to stay behind for a couple reasons. First, Lee would be able to get there MUCH faster without a slowpoke along. And second, it was the first time I had a chance to stop on the side of the road. All the other times we stopped were at restaurants or in towns. I wanted to take in the environment of the countryside.

It was relaxing. There was a pond on the other side of the fence, which Del helpfully named "crocodile lake". He pointed out clumps of floating logs that could have been crocodiles...but weren't. Phew. Across the highway were some cultivated fields.

Passing traffic was sparse. It was quiet, and the air was humid and warming noticeably.

We named this pond "Crocodile Lake".

The road where we stopped

Del gave me some more riding tips, and I asked if he could take me two-up on the yellow bike on the way back. I just couldn't get the advice to fall into place, and sometimes a two-up ride helps with that. Eventually, Lee and Andrea returned with the Jeep, and the poor bike was loaded.

We watched for traffic as Lee backed out the trailer onto the road then I climbed onto the passenger seat on the GSXR. We quickly passed the Jeep and wound our way through the curves. Ahhhh...now THIS is what a bike is supposed to feel like! Smooth and controlled. I was completely relaxed, though we were going much faster than I went solo. Not pushing it at all, just cruising. All too soon, we were out of the hills and back to the flatland.

Sitting around the kitchen table back at the house, it dawned on me that this was the first time I had ridden two-up on the street since Mike's accident. My eyes filled with tears as I shared this with Andrea. I really miss it.

The afternoon was quiet, just relaxing around the house for me. Andrea and Del went out in the canoe, where he finally achieved his goal of rounding the buoy and riding the waves with the surfers. It was a better day for water adventures since it wasn't as windy.

Dinner that night was with Gilberto and his wife, Lourdes, at their restaurant. Good food, and lots of it! After we finished eating, Lourdes sat down with us and told stories. Her Spanish was so fast and used such extensive vocabulary that I missed most of it, but it didn't matter because she was so animated, she had us all laughing with her dramatic delivery. It was a good night.

After dinner, I saw a glimpse of the sunset, and Gilberto told me how to get to the ocean. I hopped up from the dinner table

and quickly walked the two blocks to the beach. After snapping
a few photos, I strolled back to the restaurant through the warm,
humid night, with the streets slowly waking to what nightlife
there was.

Day Five:

Barra de Navidad

Today was our rest day. No riding scheduled for today. Andrea and Del spent the morning snorkeling with Gilberto. Lee
was busy cutting the grass at the town entrance all morning, his
volunteer work. Christine was working on the town's historic
mural.

I spent a couple hours walking around town and taking photos. It was nice to spend a bit of time alone, to wander the empty
morning streets and stop to check out anything that struck my
fancy. The town was deserted, except for the few shops that
were open and the gringo surfers at the malecon.

The malecon, Barra de Navidad, Mexico

In the afternoon, I curled up with a book on a lounge chair in the backyard. Taking a break from reading to gaze out over the canal, I felt warm and languid and slow. I hadn't thought about home for days. My house, work, the dark winter...it all seemed hazy and indistinct.

Thinking about home, I realized that I didn't have any more plans for the future - not that mattered, at least. Since the accident, I've made it through by moving from one goal to the next. The thought of continuing on, the thought of the future...it just made me sigh. It made me weary, like a chore that will never end. I put the thought out of my mind. "I am here now; tomorrow will take care of itself."

For dinner, we went to Martin's Restaurant in Melaque. It's a wonderful, cozy, open-air restaurant with very good food. Yet again, Lee and Christine knew the owner. Everywhere we went, they greeted people by name, knew the proprietors of the establishments and people on the streets. It made the country feel very friendly.

The view from Martin's Restaurant, Melaque, Mexico.

Day Six:

Barra de Navidad to Pérula

Today was the first day that Del and I rode without Lee. His back was hurting too much to ride. We decided to go to Pérula, our aborted destination when the chain fell off. Setting off, I felt like I was finally getting into a bit of a good groove.

Instead of being scary obstacles, the topes (speedbumps) were fun. Del took it easy, and I was able to almost completely relax on the ride. I wasn't using the brakes in every turn and was much smoother on the throttle. I'm not sure if I was actually riding better, was getting used to the GSXR finally, or it was simply that Del was riding really slowly. Whatever the reason, I thoroughly enjoyed the ride out. The highway was still green and lush and beautiful; the bike felt good; and it was fun to have a new destination for the day.

A little over an hour later, we made it to Pérula, where we crossed the town and turned onto a dirt road towards the beach. This dirt road was a different experience for me. It seemed to be covered with mini moguls, not potholes but small smooth bumps. I just kept the throttle steady and tried to pick the smoothest path through. Kind of fun but also kind of "whoa!"

The road ends here. Pérula, Mexico

The road ended at the beach, where we parked. I pulled off my helmet and took a few photos as Del walked ahead and disappeared down the little hill. His voice drifted back to me..."Wow." I quickly followed, curious to see what prompted that response. As I rounded the top of the hill, I echoed him.

"Wow."

The beach was stunning. We were the only people at the restaurant, our table on the sand. As we ate breakfast, we watched the pelicans and other birds we couldn't name. They walked in the surf, bobbed in the waves, and flew above, diving for their breakfast. The sun glittered off the water and illuminated fish in the curl of the waves. I was very tempted to run into the water. It was ideal. I could have spent all day there.

Coming over the rise, we were greeted by this view. Pérula, Mexico

Birds feeding, Pérula, Mexico

Near the end of lunch, I decided to check the time on the satellite tracker. I patted the pocket...hmmm...too flat. I reached in and my heart sank. The pocket was open and the tracker was gone. Worse, when I checked the rest of my pockets, Christine's cell phone was gone too. I never lose things. I couldn't believe it.

We started back to the house, and I had to wrench my mind back to the road. I was so frustrated with myself. I had to remind myself that losing their phone was one thing. It would be far worse to mess up the bike. Time to pay attention.

I really thought we had a decent chance of spotting the bright yellow tracker. The phone was a small, silver flip phone so I wasn't as optimistic on that score. But...we didn't find either.

Pulling into the house, I confessed my sin to Christine, and she was very gracious about it. Luckily, the tracking function of the satellite tracker was turned on so we were able to look it up on the online map. I was curious to see if it would be moving (meaning that someone picked it up), but no, it was stationary. Unfortunately, it was almost all the way back to Pérula. Zooming in and out on the map, we were able to pinpoint the location, just past a long, concrete bridge.

Del and Andrea were kind enough to offer to look for it with me so we hopped in the car and headed back. We found the stretch of road where it should have been and walked both sides of the road...but no luck. The tracker (and phone) could have been right next to the road, but the foliage was so thick, it was impossible to see anything beneath it. Oh well. At least I have a good story for how I lost the dang thing!

On the way back, we stopped at the beach in Tenacatita. I sat on a log in the sun and took some photos while Andrea and Del climbed the rocks around the far end of the beach. Finally, I just sat and watched the waves.

I missed Mike. He would have loved this whole experience. He would have loved the riding. He would have been paddling to Melaque with Del. He would have jumped up to help with the bike maintenance. He would have fit into our little group perfectly. Of course, logically, I know that if he was still alive, we wouldn't be here. I wouldn't have pushed my riding so hard last year. I wouldn't have reached out to Lee. But see, the logic didn't matter. I just wished he was here.

Playa Tenacatita at low tide, Mexico

Back at the house, Christine was glazing the rum cake she had made. It smelled amazing! We changed and went outside to pile into the car for dinner, when we saw the police driving down the street. This was the second time today that we ran into them as we were walking out of the house. They stopped and got out of the patrol truck to say hi.

As we stood in a circle talking, Christine mentioned that I would be leaving tomorrow. Officer A., who I had met at lunch earlier in the week, came up with question after question about when I would be returning. In six months? In February? For Christmas?

Eventually, we headed off for dinner. As we drove away, Lee said to me, "Candiya!" (I always imagined an exclamation point after my name when he said it.) "There's one good thing that's come out of your visit!"

"What's that?" I asked.

"We've never had so many police patrols before. They've

been up and down our street five times today!"

We went out to dinner in Melaque. The view was gorgeous, like a Hollywood movie set.

Melaque, Mexico

Driving home through the warm, tropical darkness, we told stories, and our laughter rocked the Jeep and spilled out into the night. Back at home, we lingered over the rum cake, as I avoided packing. I couldn't believe the week was ending already.

Day Seven:

Barra de Navidad to Tenacatita to Bremerton, Washington

This was the first morning of the trip that I woke early enough to join the regular morning dog walk, which happened daily at 5:30 am. We walked the dark neighborhood with the dogs. Returning to the house, we drank coffee and chatted around the kitchen table. Seized by an impulse, I brought up the photo threads of Mike to share. "I know I've been talking about him this week so I thought you might like to see him." We scrolled through the photos as I told the stories behind them.

My flight wasn't until the afternoon so we had time for one final ride in the morning. I asked Del if he'd take me two-up. I'd been good this week, stepped up and challenged my fears. This was my reward. Riding two-up doesn't provide the sense of accomplishment of riding my own. But still, I love it. I'd say it's pure pleasure, but it's more like 90% pleasure and 10% "damn, my knees hurt." (At 5'10", there's no way around the fact that I'm not built to be a sport bike passenger.)

We headed off to Tenacatita on the green bike. That bike is a monster! Certainly no lack of power there. We stopped for another break at the same restaurant as the first day. My wrists, triceps, and knees appreciated the chance to stretch, but I had a grin a mile wide. After a quick break, we returned to the house. The ride back felt fast and smooth. What a treat for my last ride in Mexico.

Stopping for a break near Tenacatita, Mexico

Back home in the garage. Yippee - I made it through the week without dropping the yellow bike! (Gotta celebrate the little things.)

For lunch today, we decided to grab a water taxi and eat at the resort across the water. Before taking the taxi, we stopped to complete an errand: buying Christine a new phone.

It was another beautiful ride across the water, and it was interesting to see the resort's pools up close. As we sat down at the table by the pool, I looked around. All of the resort guests seemed to be from the US, and the only language I heard was English. I was so grateful for the Mexican experience that I had had this week: meeting Lee and Christine's Mexican friends and hearing their stories, eating at restaurants where the staff didn't speak English, and the food was authentic. A resort vacation would have been beautiful and relaxing, but it wouldn't have provided the rich cultural experience of staying with these new friends. I felt very lucky.

At the resort, Barra de Navidad, Mexico

After lunch, it was time to gather up my bags and head to the airport. I hugged Lee and Andrea goodbye, and Christine, Del, and I hopped in the car. As we drove, Christine said that she was sad to see me go, that I had been a successful mystery guest. That made me feel good. I had tried not to be too intrusive or a burden and to be a good guest. I felt a true friendship with them and hoped it was returned. Christine walked me into the airport, and all too soon, it was time to say goodbye.

Landing in Los Angeles

Like on the way down, my layover was in Los Angeles. I stood in line for Customs, and the agent called me up and asked, "What were you doing in Mexico?"

Holding up my helmet with a big smile, I said, "Riding motorcycles!"

He laughed and responded, "Oh, you're one of THOSE women!"

I laughed too. "Yes, but I'm not sure what that means. What does it mean?"

"You're out there doing things. Like Nike, 'just do it!'"

"Well, yes. I'm still afraid, but I do it anyways."

He smiled, handed my passport back, and waved me on my way.

After dinner at the airport, I boarded the flight back to Seattle. As we took off on the last leg of the trip home, I reflected on what I had learned in the past week. Perhaps this diary entry says it best:

Sitting in the Manzanillo airport boarding area, my heart is full and empty at the same time. I want to cry. Saying goodbye to Christine and the crew was so hard! Now I am sitting here feeling simultaneously blessed, incredibly blessed, and weary and afraid to pick up the daily round again. This has been an incredible interlude.

If I am looking for reasons to choose life, this trip has reminded me of some dear ones: the fact that there are good people in the world, who welcome strangers into their home and show them a new culture, introduce them to their friends, and share the richness of their lives. Green and beautiful highways with new friends to lead the way. Adventure and exploration. Pushing my limits, stretching myself so that the new me will be able to reach beyond my boundaries.

I am starting from scratch in constructing a life. Step-by-step, I will get there.

Leaving Los Angeles, heading home

A few weeks before the trip, someone had posted a thread on one of the motorcycle forums; in response to the documentary film *Why We Ride*, the thread asked, "Why do you ride?"

I've struggled to articulate the answer to this question since the accident. When people, especially non-riders, find out that I still ride, a look of pity and incomprehension passes over their faces. I never know how to respond. When I posted in the thread, this is what came out:

> *I ride for the sensation.*
>
> *I ride for the community.*
>
> *I ride because challenging my fears reminds me that I'm alive.*
>
> *I ride because, while I can talk to my lost love anytime, it's the one time I know he's listening.*

This is why I did the trip to Mexico - for the riding itself, for the community, for the challenge, and because it's a way that I could honor Mike while reaching for something new. The phrase "moving on" is so difficult because it implies moving away. It implies distance. Maybe this was a way that I could "move forward" instead, while carrying him with me.

When I stood in front of the crowd at the memorial service to deliver the eulogy, I read from a prepared statement. The eulogy had been written in advance, except for the last line, which came out of me as I spoke. While it wasn't on the page, I couldn't hold it back when I reached the end. The last line was, "I will carry him in my heart forever." And that statement is just as true today.

It's not about being wedded to the past but about carrying that love forward, as I move forward. As I said in the introduction to the first ride report, I want this year to be about choosing life. This Mexico trip was a step towards finding that new life.

CHAPTER 71

Accident day

March 6, 2014

I should have written this long ago but was afraid to face it. I've already forgotten some details, and the memory of the day now feels hazy and distant, which is both a blessing and another sadness. Here, finally, is the story of the accident day. This is not the story of the accident. I was not there. This is the story of my experience on that fateful day.

The week after the accident, I was afraid of forgetting Mike's last day alive, our last day together. One night when I couldn't sleep, I wrote down bullet points of remembrance. Below is part of that list, starting with me picking him up at the airport, when he arrived home after three and a half months at sea. This was the last deployment of his career so this arrival was more than just a homecoming; it was the beginning of the rest of our lives together. Our relationship would no longer to be marred by spending months apart.

The list is titled "Memories":

- After picking Mike up at the airport, he stopped to give me several good kisses before getting in the truck.

- Mike's bike was in the back of the truck. After we got onto Highway 90, he started rooting through the center console asking me where the key to the bike was. I teased him that it didn't matter, that Buz could just hotwire it every morning. Mike said no, that we should turn around before we got too far and that the bike couldn't be hotwired. Then I showed him the bike key sitting under my house keys in the cup holder, and he laughed.

- He rode most of the day sitting wonky in the passenger seat so that he could touch and stroke my leg.

- At one point, I opened my water bottle, and water squirted out on my shirt and leg. With a big grin, he solicitously leaned over with napkins to feel me up as he dried me off.

- He researched restaurants as I drove so that we could stop and have a good lunch.

- He researched motorcycle shops as I drove, and we stopped at a couple to find some new gloves for him – summer weight – since I hadn't found his white ones to bring.

- He had booked a room at the Geiser Grand hotel so that both of us could have our first night together in a nice place. For me, it was a thank you for making his motorcycle road trip happen, and for him, it was a night of luxury after getting off the boat.

Geiser Grand Hotel: Our last night together

- At the hotel that evening, he waffled about whether or not to order a drink, going so far as to ask me to call the front desk to see if room service could deliver a Jack and Coke. Ultimately, he decided that it wouldn't be a good idea so he skipped it.

- We went to sleep around 10:00 pm. We spent the night snuggling, wrapped around each other.
- The next morning we were up and ready to go by 6:50. We loaded the bags in the truck and down went to breakfast. I didn't enjoy mine, but Mike liked his and ate well.
- During breakfast, Mike commented on how he had been afraid that he'd be dragging, but he felt really good. He looked bright-eyed and energetic.
- Over breakfast, we talked about options for our vacation, which was to come after his motorcycle trip. I told him that I wanted a night or two together, followed by a motorcycle trip of our own. He suggested that we drive up to Port Angeles and take the ferry to Victoria. After a couple nights there, we could return to Washington and take the bikes over the mountains of Highway 20, for my first time riding that route on my own bike.
- After breakfast, we drove a couple blocks to the motel where his friends had stayed the night. Mike joined them as they prepped in the parking lot, laughing and joking with each other. It was pretty funny watching them figure out the Bluetooth helmet-to-helmet communicators. They'd touch the helmets/communicators together then walk around the parking lot repeating, "Can you hear me now?"
- As they finalized their preparations, Mike stopped to give me a really good kiss. After he put on his helmet, we laughed and pantomimed another kiss.

The "Memories" document stopped at this point. Below is the rest of the story...

I took a photo of the guys, and then they rolled out. A few minutes later, I hit the road myself in the truck, heading back home to Bremerton. I passed them a block later at the gas station, and we waved at each other. That was the last time I saw Mike alive.

I started the drive back home from Baker City. Gradually, the nerves of homecoming dissipated, and while I missed him like crazy, I was in a good mood. The sun was out, and I was singing along with the country station when I heard my phone chime. This was about an hour and twenty minutes into the drive, and I was negotiating some hills just before Pendleton. I glanced at the phone and saw that I'd missed a call from Mike's friend, Mark. The chime that I'd heard was the voicemail notification.

Immediately, I had a bad feeling. Why would Mark call now? I told myself, "I need to pull over before listening to this voicemail." There was no shoulder on the highway, but there was an exit a short way ahead. I took the exit and pulled into the rest stop parking lot.

I called my voicemail and heard Mark's halting voice. He told me that Mike had been in an accident, and "he didn't make it." I remember that phrase clearly. He asked me to call him back and closed by saying, "This isn't a joke." Immediately, I seized upon that last sentence. Maybe it was just a joke! Though I knew that they would never joke about something like this, especially with me. Adrenaline was coursing through my veins. I was shaking and felt nauseous. I was ready to fly into action.

I called Mark. "What happened?" My voice was small and sounded distant in my own ears. I wasn't crying. In fact, I thought I sounded way *too* calm. Mark explained that Mike had missed a turn. I remember asking, "There's nothing that can be done?" "No," he said helplessly. He told me that Mike had no pulse. I flinched away from the image. He asked me to come to them, and when I asked where they were, my brain couldn't process how to look it up on a map.

I hung up and tried to pull myself together to drive. The nausea was overwhelming. I opened the door to the truck, and as I slid out of the driver's seat, I said out loud, "I knew it was too good to last." This relationship that Mike and I had, it wasn't a new infatuation. We had taken our time and slowly built something that was so much better than I had ever thought possible. We were about five years in.

I slowly walked into the rest stop, intent on making it to the restroom before I threw up. As I stood in the bathroom stall, I coached myself: "You are not truly sick. Throwing up will not make you feel better. You probably won't be able to eat for a while so don't throw up if you don't have to. Conserve your strength and your fuel." I didn't throw up. I washed my hands and exited the bathroom.

There was a little metal bench between the men's and women's restrooms, and I lowered myself onto it. I watched the people walking by, and my eyes beseeched them. I was looking for someone, anyone, to tell me that it wasn't true. A woman stopped in front of me. "Are you okay?" she asked. "No," I responded. "I just got some bad news." I couldn't say the bad news out loud. That would make it too real. "Would you mind if I prayed for you?" she asked. "Yes, please," I answered. I thought she'd continue on her way and add me to her prayers that night...but no.

She walked up and put her arm around me, and she started to pray out loud. Her words washed over me. She prayed for the Lord to give me strength to face what I needed to. I don't remember everything she said, but I remember being flattened with gratitude. Eventually, her prayer came to an end. She asked if there was anything else she could do for me. I had such an ugly taste in my mouth; I really wanted a cold bottle of water to sip, but I had left my purse in the truck and didn't have any cash. I was too shy to ask her for water without giving her money to cover it.

The next set of memories float around my brain like loose little bubbles. They aren't grounded in any sort of linear progression. But I remember...

Another phone call with the guys where they told me not to come after all. They didn't want me to see Mike like this. They told me that the highway patrol would be calling me soon.

The rest stop was set up with a parking lot for passenger cars and a parking lot for big rigs, with a little grassy area and a couple small trees in between. Still trying to get my nausea under control, I floated between the truck, the rest stop market (where I bought a bottle of water), and that grassy patch. I sat on the grass under the little tree, just sat there and watched the cars coming and going and the people climbing out of their vehicles to stretch. The couples and families laughed and joked and passed before me as they walked into the rest stop. They seemed distant and foreign, aliens from another planet that I had left and couldn't return to. Sometimes they saw me, and I'm sure I looked very strange. Most of the time, I was invisible.

I waited for the highway patrol to call. I grasped that thought and held onto it. That call would make it all better. This would be an official, someone who really knew what was going on. He would tell me it wasn't true. About 40 minutes later, the call came in. The officer's voice was gentle and sympathetic; there was nothing "official" or hard about it. He asked how Mike had gotten there, and I explained how he had returned from deployment yesterday morning. I described how I had picked him up in the truck with the bike loaded in the back, and we had met up with his friends in Baker City, where we spent the night. That morning, I had dropped him off with the guys, and he rode off with them as I started my trip back home in the truck. I told him that since Mike was active duty military, someone would need to be called, but I had no idea who. I had no Navy phone numbers and knew no one from his boat.

He asked if I had any contact information for his family, and I said yes, his mom. He asked if I had called her yet and was surprised when I said no. I felt a crushing sense of shame. I was supposed to call her? I didn't know. Plus, why would I call when I had been waiting for the officials to tell me that it wasn't true? He asked if I wanted to call her or if I'd like him to. I thought a moment, as I imagined the different scenarios. No, she should find out from me. I would call. He said he'd wait 10 minutes to give me a chance to call her first. Before we hung up, I interrupted him. "Could I just ask you a question?" "Sure," he answered. "Could you just tell me...is this real? Did this really happen?" A moment of silence, then his sympathetic voice. "Yes, I'm so sorry. It's very real." I thanked him and hung up.

I sat on that patch of grass and stared at my phone. What would I say to his mom? How do you tell a mother that her son is dead? I pressed her contact information to dial her number and listened to her phone ring. "Oh no, her voicemail," I thought in a panic. "Don't make me leave this in a voicemail." But I did. I left a voicemail very similar to the one Mark left for me. A couple minutes later, she called me back. Her voice sounded warm and comforting. "What's wrong, honey?" She hadn't been able to hear the message so I told her. Mike had been in an accident, and he didn't make it. I was so sorry. The highway patrol would be calling her soon. And I distinctly re-member saying to her, "I wish you were here." I didn't know his parents well since they lived across the country. But truer words had never been spoken. I wished she were sitting on the grass beside me. "I wish I were too," she said.

Now that I had confirmation that it was real (though I still didn't believe it), I knew that I should call someone for help. My heart quailed at the thought of driving home. There were still roughly six hours of highway ahead, plus the added obstacle of Seattle-area traffic. I could have bucked up and made that drive, but I knew that it would have been a bad idea. I wandered back inside the rest stop, visited the restroom again and settled on the bench. I couldn't figure out who to call. The only person who came to mind was Mike. In my mind's eye, I flipped through a list of different people. My friends and family in California were too far away to help. My mom has difficulty driving long dis-tances; plus, I couldn't face calling her yet. Finally, I settled on my friend, Dionne.

I pressed her contact information and listened to the phone ring on the other end, crossing my fingers that her voicemail wouldn't pick up. She answered. "Hi, doll! What's up?" she chirped, with a smile in her voice. "Hi Dionne, it's Candiya," I said. I tried to order my thoughts, but my mind was blank. I listened with curiosity to see what would come out of my mouth next. "I'm in trouble," I said. A rush of relief. Yes, that was ex-actly the right thing to say. I *was* in trouble.

I explained the situation. I was in Oregon. I had dropped Mike off with the guys and had gotten a call from his friend saying that he had been in an accident, and he didn't make it. "Wait," she interrupted. "Mike??" "Yes," I said impatiently. In my mind, I was calling with a logistical problem - how to get myself and the truck home. It didn't occur to me that I was also delivering some tragic news. I regret that I was not gentler. She gasped a few sobs, and then got herself under control. We talked for a bit. She told me that she would work on arranging everything and would call me back.

As we texted back and forth, it became clear that it would make a lot more sense time-wise to ask Mike's friends to come get me. Plus, I wanted to see them. They had been there in person. They knew the truth. They would tell me that it wasn't real. I texted them. "I am not good to drive. Could someone come get me when you can?" It went against the grain to ask for help, but I could not do this alone. (Just one of the many lessons from this loss.) They responded that they would come as soon as they were done at the accident site, but it would take about three hours of travel time for them to make it to me. That was fine. I didn't mind waiting. Waiting was better than the alternative, trying to figure out where I should be and what I should do - when there was nowhere to go and nothing to do that would make it better.

I spent the next several hours sitting on the grass beneath my little tree. When I tell people this, they look at me with pity, perhaps even with horror, as they picture me sitting in a parking lot alone, for hours after receiving this news. But in reality, I am grateful for that patch of grass and little tree and time alone. The thought of the alternative, getting the news at home, being so far away from the accident and consumed with a pure need to DO something, while being trapped in my house with people talking at me and hugging me... I can't even picture it without my chest tightening.

If there was nowhere to be that would make it better, my little patch of grass was just fine. I sat there and sipped my water.

I brought the newspaper out of the truck, thinking that I would read, but I couldn't focus for more than a paragraph. My thoughts dulled further, and I closed my eyes and slipped into sleep for a little while, the scratchy blades of grass poking my cheek and leaving their brand when I woke, and the soft warm breeze brushing the skin on my arm. I felt ashamed when I woke. My boyfriend was dead, and here I was sleeping. I vowed never to admit this to anyone. Today, I know that it was the shock, and I forgive myself for the nap.

I knew that I should have been hungry, though the thought of food was revolting. Still, I wandered inside and purchased a small box of Wheat Thins. I managed to eat two, with small, mincing bites. The crackers turned to dust in my mouth as I chewed. Mostly, I just sat and watched...the grass, the people, the cars and the big rigs. I watched and waited and tried not to think.

I was laying on the grass when I heard the bikes pull in. I opened my eyes and looked up between two parked cars. Buz walked through that space, the speed hump on the back of the motorcycle jacket giving him a distinctive silhouette. I gathered myself together and walked out to meet them. Everything seemed to move in slow motion. There were only three bikes. Mike's was not there.

We stood in the parking lot, and when I asked what happened, they told me the story of the accident. We talked about next steps, and they loaded Buz's bike into the truck so he could drive me home. I sent the other two riders off with fervent requests to be safe on the ride back.

I felt sorry for Buz, stuck driving me. This was the start of me feeling sorry for anyone "stuck" being with me. It's hard to explain why. It some ways, I felt that being with me made his death real to those around me, in the same way that visiting someone in the hospital makes their illness real. I also felt that I was a burden on those around me. Everyone was awkward around me, and it made me feel like I should apologize. Their lives would be easier if they weren't with me, a living embodiment of the death.

On the drive home, I simply sat and watched the landscape roll by, trying not to think of what was waiting at the other end. The drive was punctuated by texts from Mike's mom, keeping me apprised of the official side of things. Her matter-of-fact texts about the organ donation were shocking. Didn't they realize that they were making a mistake? He couldn't be dead. Dionne had asked if I wanted her to call our mutual friends and notify them, and I had said yes. On the drive, texts started to trickle in as people heard the news. I dreaded posting his RIP thread in the motorcycle forum.

I asked Buz to take me to my mom's place (the extended stay hotel where she was staying), and he dropped me off and took the truck home. I had called my mom from Baker City so she knew we were coming. She gave me a huge hug and asked if she could make me anything. I asked for a smoothie, thinking that I might be able to get that down. I was able to finish about half of it. I logged onto the motorcycle forum and saw that another friend had posted Mike's RIP thread, much more eloquently than I could have managed. I was so relieved not to have to face drafting it myself.

I called Dionne, and she came to pick me up at my mom's hotel. The thought of going home made me feel panicky and horror-filled. Going back to our home without him...I just couldn't face it. Dionne and her husband, Tom, invited me to stay with them, and I took them up on it for two nights.

At their house, Dionne asked if she could make me anything, and one of the items she listed was Mexican hot chocolate. That sounded perfect. She shaved the chocolate into the milk and heated it up. It was warm and smooth and filling. We sat on her couches and talked until the dullness started to encroach upon my thoughts again. "I think I'll be able to sleep now," I told them and excused myself. I crawled into bed and read a magazine to short circuit my brain from thinking. I quickly dropped into sleep and managed to sleep for a few hours before the panic began to grow and grow in my chest. I had to get out of bed and make tea while I waited for the panic to subside. This was to become my nightly ritual. I would fall asleep early, as if I were sedated (though I refused all medication), then I would wake in a growing panic until I pulled myself out of bed, read, drank tea, and waited until I got tired enough to go back to sleep.

And so began my new life. Day one post-accident. Day one with everything I knew about the world and myself shattered. Day one of the new me.

And so began my journey. A journey that started in absolute despair, in darkness, in a jungle of pain and desperation. With no path before me, I began to feel my way out, like a blind woman. There was no guarantee that I would survive this journey, yet I knew that to remain still would be certain death. A death of the spirit. The only choice was to move. And so, in this strange and scary new world, I closed my eyes and trusted my gut. Like metal shavings pulled from one lodestone to the next, I began to take step by careful step through the darkness. Though I could not explain to anyone, much less myself, why I took each step, in retrospect, each was necessary. Each played a role in pulling me out of the depths.

This journey has taken me to destinations and sights I never could have imagined, from the broad, sweeping sky above the Oregon sage plain where Mike met his end; to the quiet stillness of the Kansas cemetery where he rests today; the racetrack surrounded by the orange, craggy mountains of Utah; the chill breezes of the California coast; the moist damp earth scent of the giant redwoods; and finally, the twisty, serpentine highways through the jungles of Mexico. This journey has taken me through every emotion imaginable, intensely and thoroughly, overlaid atop one another and sequentially, through cycles and spirals.

In the midst of it all, it was difficult to see any progress. But now, yes, I can see how far I have come. The journey is not over, by any means. There is still healing to be found. But now, a year and a half into this journey, a year into the writing, this is a good time to stop and take stock, to celebrate the gains, to celebrate the fact that I made it here today.

Last week, I read an article in the *New York Times*; it was an interview with a woman whose parents had survived the Holocaust. A quote from the article resonated with me like a bell struck in my heart: "Growing up in a community of survivors left her permanently thinking about how people find their way to vibrant lives. 'In my community there were two groups of people,' she said. 'There were the ones who did not die and the ones who came back to life.'"

It is a choice. I choose to fight to come back to life. There are no guarantees, of any sort. No guarantees of safety on the road, no guarantees that I will find my way to a vibrant life. But if the choice is between being one "who did not die" and one "who came back to life"...

I choose life.

Endnotes

Eulogy and photos

An introduction: eulogy

This book is about me, but I thought that you might like to know something about Mike too. Here, then, is an introduction. Endings as beginnings, in so many ways. What better way for me to introduce Mike than to share the eulogy I read at his memorial service?

After the accident, I knew that I wanted to speak at the service, though I had no idea if I'd be able to organize my thoughts well enough to prepare anything. I postponed the writing until the last minute. The service was scheduled for a Wednesday. I sat down on the prior sunny Sunday morning to try to write, at least to write a paragraph. I did write that paragraph, and in fact, the entire eulogy in one sitting. It flowed out of me in a single piece.

There are hidden messages within it: notes of acknowledgement to our friends that they mattered to him. My goal was to be a storyteller, in the most sacred, historic tradition of storytellers. My goal was to bring him to life through my words and remembrances. My goal was to share a peek into the treasure that he was. He didn't see himself as anything special, but I knew better.

Dear reader, please meet Mike:

Eulogy

When thinking about what to write, I realized that it's impossible to recount the entirety of Mike's life, our relationship, or what made him special. In lieu of that, I thought I'd share a few memories that make me smile.

In 2010, we did a motorcycle road trip to Vancouver Island. We spent a couple days in Tofino and went kayaking. We set off one gorgeous morning – just the two of us with our guide - and paddled to a couple of islands where we hiked through old growth forest. In the afternoon, the wind picked up, whitecaps appeared, and it started to look a little dangerous. The trip was cut short as all of the guides and guests who were on the water at the time gathered in a protected cove and strategized how to get back safely.

We crossed the open water together in a group, though the guide kept having to tell Mike to wait up because he was powering ahead through the whitecaps. It was a tense crossing through the open water. When we made it to shore, I breathed a huge sigh of relief. Mike? He turned around with a HUGE grin and sparkling eyes and said, "That was GREAT!"

Hiking old growth forest, Tofino, British Columbia, July 2010

He loved adventures and new experiences, big and small. On the small side, whenever we went out to eat, I could reliably guess what he would order because he'd always pick the strangest, most oddball meal on the menu or the beer he'd never tried before.

Farewell sushi with friends before he went out to sea, November 2010. Photo credit: Jane Carter Courtney.

Mike nearly always accomplished what he set his mind to. In 2011, he completed the Big Sur Marathon, one of the most challenging courses in North America. This would be impressive enough if you didn't know the rest of the story, which is that this was his first marathon, and because he had been out to sea until shortly before the race, his longest training run was only eight miles. He completed the 26.2 miles by force of will alone.

Big Sur Marathon, May 2011

He enjoyed being physically active, and he enjoyed helping people. Often, these two traits came into play together, like when he volunteered for beach clean-up, trail building, and helping friends at their oyster farm and building a boat house. The beach clean-up was funny. About three-quarters down the beach, we came across a giant tractor tire. Mike went for it. The whole group of friends kept telling him that he'd never get it up the hill to the dumpster so he might as well leave it, but he just rolled it down the beach with a grin on his face. Of course, I'm sure you can guess the end of this story. Mike manhandled that huge tire - not only across the beach - but up a muddy, steep trail, over a tree that had fallen across the trail, and all the way to the dumpster. And of course he had a smile the whole time.

He loved being out in nature. I asked him once why he liked riding motorcycles, and one of the reasons he gave was that you never knew when you were going to come around a bend and find another glorious view. Those were his words, "glorious view". It's not too often you find a guy who uses the word "glorious" in casual conversation.

Hiking Garrapata State Park, Big Sur, California, November 2008. Photo credit: Christina Watson

About six months after I met Mike, I told him that he was a good man. In response, he looked really sad and dropped his head. I thought, "Hmmm…this isn't the reaction I was expecting." It turns out that he thought I was saying he was a "good guy" and that I was trying to let him down easy. That wasn't the case at all. He WAS a good man, and all his actions in the following years supported it. Mike was honest, full of integrity, loyal, dependable, funny, silly, generous, strong, gentle, protective, kind, and loving.

I will carry him in my heart forever.

Photos

Here are some of my favorite photos of us.

Exploring the Bloedel Reserve, Bainbridge, Washington, August 2009

Scrunching to fit the photo booth at the Rottweiler Bikes Garage Party, June 2011. Photo credit: Rottweiler Bikes

Celebrating a friend's birthday, April 2011. Photo credit: Elizabeth Tailleur

Celebrating Halloween 2009, as Elvis and Cleopatra. Photo credit: Jane Carter Courtney

Hiking the Hoh Rainforest, Washington, February 2012

Hiking the Hood Canal, 2008

Goodbye, my love.

About the Author

Photo credit: Dan Carratturo

Candiya Mann does social science research and program evaluations for National Science Foundation grant recipients. She lives in Bremerton, Washington, in a little house full of houseplants, with a little garage full of motorcycles. Someday, she will get a dog.

Made in the USA
Charleston, SC
25 November 2016